633053

W9-BLC-166

FRANKLIN REGIONAL
SENIOR HIGH
LIBRARY

THEotherAMERICA

Teens with DISABILITIES

by Gail B. Stewart

Photographs by
Carl Franzén

Lucent Books, P.O. Box 289011, San Diego, CA 92198-9011

These and other titles are included in *The Other America* series:

Battered Women	Teen Alcoholics
Gangs	Teen Dropouts
Gay and Lesbian Youth	Teen Fathers
The Homeless	Teen Mothers
Homeless Teens	Teen Runaways
Illegal Immigrants	Teens in Prison
People with AIDS	Teens with Disabilties
Teen Addicts	Teens with Eating Disorders

Cover design: Carl Franzén

Library of Congress Cataloging-in-Publication Data

Stewart, Gail 1949-
    Teens with disabilities / by Gail B. Stewart.
        p. cm.—(The other America)
    Includes bibliographical references and index.
    Summary: Profiles four teenagers with disabilities, discussing their
problems and the ways with which they have dealt with their disabilities.
    ISBN 1-56006-815-9

The opinions of and stories told by the people in this book are entirely their own. The author has presented their accounts in their own words and has not verified their accuracy. Thus, the author can make no claim as to the objectivity of their accounts.

No part of this book may be reproduced or used in any form or by any means, electrical, mechanical, or otherwise, including, but not limited to, photocopy, recording, or any information storage and retrieval system, without prior written permission from the publisher.

Printed in the U.S.A.
Copyright © 2001 by Lucent Books, Inc.
P.O. Box 289011, San Diego, CA 92198-9011

Contents

Foreword

O, YES,
I SAY IT PLAIN,
AMERICA NEVER WAS AMERICA TO ME.
AND YET I SWEAR THIS OATH—
AMERICA WILL BE!
    LANGSTON HUGHES

Perhaps more than any other nation in the world, the United States represents an ideal to many people. The ideal of equality—of opportunity, of legal rights, of protection against discrimination and oppression. To a certain extent, this image has proven accurate. But beneath this ideal lies a less idealistic fact—many segments of our society do not feel included in this vision of America.

They are the outsiders—the homeless, the elderly, people with AIDS, teenage mothers, gang members, prisoners, and countless others. When politicians and the media discuss society's ills, the members of these groups are defined as what's wrong with America; they are the people who need fixing, who need help, or increasingly, who need to take more responsibility. And as these people become society's fix-it problem, they lose all identity as individuals and become part of an anonymous group. In the media and in our minds these groups are identified by condition—a disease, crime, morality, poverty. Their condition becomes their identity, and once this occurs, in the eyes of society, they lose their humanity.

The Other America series reveals the members of these groups as individuals. Through in-depth interviews, each person tells his or her unique story. At times these stories are painful, revealing individuals who are struggling to maintain their integrity, their humanity, their lives, in the face of fear, loss, and economic and spiritual hardship. At other times, their tales are exasperating,

4

demonstrating a litany of poor choices, shortsighted thinking, and self-gratification. Nevertheless, their identities remain distinct, their personalities diverse.

As we listen to the people of *The Other America* series describe their experiences, they cease to be stereotypically defined and become tangible, individual. In the process, we may begin to understand more profoundly and think more critically about society's problems. When politicians debate, for example, whether the homeless problem is due to a poor economy or lack of initiative, it will help to read the words of the homeless. Perhaps then we can see the issue more clearly. The family who finds itself temporarily homeless because it has always been one paycheck from poverty is not the same as the mother of six who has been chronically chemically dependent. These people's circumstances are not all of one kind, and perhaps we, after all, are not so very different from them. Before we can act to solve the problems of the Other America, we must be willing to look down their path, to see their faces. And perhaps in doing so, we may find a piece of ourselves as well.

Introduction

Lynn, seventeen, was born with cerebral palsy, a condition that has weakened her muscles so much that she uses a wheelchair most of the time. "I can walk for short distances if I have my braces on," she explains. "But I'm slow and kind of unpredictable. Sometimes I'm okay, but sometimes I fall. So I feel more comfortable in my chair."

SET APART

Unlike some individuals born with cerebral palsy, Lynn has not suffered mental retardation or blindness; she does well academically in her high school and expects to graduate in the top third of her class next year. But while Lynn has achieved a great deal, she says that she still feels separated from others her age.

"I think it's part of the territory when you have a disability," she says. "I'm different, and so I experience different things from other kids. I'm set apart in a way. I don't think people mean to be separate or to be that way. It's just the way my life is. But if other people knew a little more about living with a disability, no matter what kind, it might be good."

NOT ALONE

Although Lynn feels isolated, statistics indicate that she is one of a large group of disabled young people in the United States. According to 1998 government statistics, more than 5.2 million Americans have some sort of disability.

Some, like Lynn, have physical problems that interfere with walking; others have vision or hearing loss. Some suffer from chronic illnesses or disease. Others have mental disabilities. Many young people have a combination of physical and mental disabilities. Experts estimate that between 10 and 12 percent of the school-age population is made up of young people with one or multiple disabilities.

"There are a great many young people in school today who have disabilities," says Marie Diaz, a Chicago counselor. "We see children entering school today who would never have survived generations ago. And they are doing so much more than surviving! With strides in technology and medicine, these kids are making great strides in education and self-sufficiency."

NOT SO MANY YEARS AGO

The status of teens with disabilities has come a long way. To be disabled has always set an individual apart; however, being born with a disability used to have tragic consequences. In ancient Greece, for example, babies born with malformed limbs or other noticeable disabilities were routinely thrown over a cliff. In other ancient cultures, such babies were buried alive at birth; occasionally, their mothers were killed as well. People did not understand disabilities or deformities and considered them an impediment to future existence.

While the cause of many disabilities has remained a mystery, people's reactions over the centuries has become less severe—although there have been great changes in the care of young people with disabilities. During the eighteenth century in the United States, for example, many believed that young disabled people were best kept at home to be cared for by family members. No surgical procedures had been developed to help them; it was simply a matter of keeping them comfortable.

In the nineteenth century, however, Americans shifted. For one thing, doctors were having some success with surgical procedures that could ease some of the most devastating effects of some disabilities. It was during this time, too, that the United States was creating a great number of institutions to handle social welfare, in large part because of the heavy influx of immigrants to this country. In addition to the hospitals, asylums, and orphanages, facilities were built to house large numbers of physically disabled people.

Disabled children could be helped in larger numbers if they were institutionalized, and that is precisely what happened. The responsibility of caring for such children and teenagers was increasingly taken out of the family's hands. In his book *Ordinary Families, Special Children: A Systems Approach to Childhood Disability,*

Milton Seligman quotes a respected 1914 study that illustrated the thinking of the day:

> That the family home is the best place for well children is now generally recognized. But crippled children are conceded to be a special class, requiring in many cases surgical operations and in many cases very close physical supervision for months, often years . . . Some surgeons insist that parents cannot be trusted to adjust a child's brace or even to bring him to the dispensary at the time ordered by the doctor.

SEEKING MORE THAN CARE

In the twentieth century, however, there has been a dramatic shift away from such institutionalization. Often alarmed by the poor conditions and staffing of large hospitals for crippled children, families were unwilling to be separated from their disabled children. But many families felt that their children needed more than simple care. As various minorities in society worked to gain equal rights and privileges (such as voting, education, and so on), parents of disabled children were more vocal about rights, too. They wanted their children to be educated and trained to live productive lives.

At first, such education was limited to special education classes, in which children with any number of disabilities were lumped together, often resulting in problems.

"I was in one of these special education classes almost forty years ago," recalls a woman who has spent most of her life in a wheelchair. "We were a mixed bag—blind kids, deaf kids, kids with really bad asthma, mentally retarded kids, and kids like me with the after-effects of polio. It must have been impossible for the teacher to get anywhere with all of us at the same time!"

BEING PART OF THE LARGER WORLD

As parents began to believe it was their right to have their child attend classes alongside their more able-bodied peers, the notion of mainstreaming gained popularity in the latter part of the twentieth century. Physically disabled students who spent more time in regular classrooms tended to have higher expectations of themselves, and as a result, did better in school.

Under such federal legislation as the 1990 Americans with Disabilities Act, and more recently, the 1997 Individuals with Disabilties

Education Act, over $3 billion per year is being allotted to schools to put disabled students in the mainstream whenever possible.

"We still get specialized help if we need it," says Laurie, a seventeen-year-old student with a spinal cord injury. "But most of my classes this year are regular classes. I like that better most of the time. It's easier to feel like I'm part of the bigger school population."

BEING A TEEN IS HARD ENOUGH

But although there have been advances in education, medicine, and technology that allow disabled youth to attend school, students with disabilities still face obstacles every day.

Says one counselor, "There are more choices today than at any time in history for teenagers with disabilities. But it is crucial to understand that in many cases, the most difficult parts of having a disability are not always the physical limitations like immobility or blindness. The social aspects, especially for a teenager, are often far more daunting."

One of the biggest obstacles is, simply put, being a teenager. More than at any time in a person's life, this is when teens seek independence, challenge parental authority, and find refuge more and more often with their peers. However, having a disability makes most of these things difficult, if not impossible.

"A teen with a physical disability is being pulled two ways," explains one high school counselor. "She wants privacy and separation occasionally from her family, yet she may need them for very personal tasks, such as using the bathroom or getting dressed. She wants to get mad occasionally, but how do you get mad at people who are doing so much for you? It's hard enough to be a teenager, but being disabled at the same time is very, very difficult."

GETTING IN THE WAY OF INDEPENDENCE

Another concern of teens with disabilities is their growing uncertainty about adult life. As children, they were nurtured and cared for by family, and like all children, were generally unconcerned about the future—a job, independent living, and even college.

"All of a sudden, I'm thinking about whether I can go to college, and if so, how I can manage it," says one teen who is a junior in high school. "I have muscular dystrophy and need breathing treatments quite often. I worry about being on my own at school. I'd like to go, but it's kind of scary thinking about it."

Teens with disabilities are also concerned about their relationships with their peers. As children who frequently spent most of their time within the family, a lack of outside socializing may have seemed unimportant. But for a teenager, time with peers is important; however, many disabled teens find it difficult to initiate such contact.

"I like a girl in my math class," says Donald, a fifteen-year-old with congenital heart disease. "But I'm absent a lot, and I miss out on things. Sometimes I feel like I don't know what kids are talking about when I come back from being gone for a week. I can keep up with homework better than I can keep up with that other stuff.

"I'd like to get to know her better, but I'm not sure if she's interested. And I can't dance or anything, so that's out. My mom says I should just call her, and maybe I'll get the courage to do that pretty soon," he says. "I know all kids go through stuff like this, not just ones with disabilities. But I think there are fewer options for us, and that makes it a little tougher."

ON THE BRIGHTER SIDE

Although teens with disabilities face many problems, some insist that they are not complaining.

"I'm grateful to be alive," says Cindy, one of the young people whose story is included in this book. "I wasn't given much of a chance to be alive past ten, and I'm almost twenty! I've got a great family and a boyfriend, and I'm thinking about college. I'm in a lot better shape than some able-bodied kids I know."

Others point to a large support base they find on the Internet.

"This wouldn't have been available to people ten or even five years ago," says one counselor. "But I talk to a lot of kids for whom the Internet is a virtual lifeline. They can tap into sites where they chat with other teens with similar situations. Even if they don't get answers to all their questions, at least they find that they're not the only ones worried about certain issues. And that helps a lot."

A CLOSER LOOK

The four young people interviewed in the following chapters are at different stages of their teenage years. Patrick, a thirteen-year-old with arthrogryposis who must use leg braces, is in seventh grade.

One of four adopted children in his family with a birth defect, he says that has helped him be brave. Still, he admits that he has real worries about being a teenager.

Dennis, fifteen, is a medical miracle. Born prematurely, he has gone through many surgeries and has logged hundreds of days in the hospital—for everything from congestive heart failure to the insertion of a head shunt. Especially close to his father, Dennis is still dealing with the fact that his mother left when he was a baby.

Cindy, just turning twenty, has a form of muscular dystrophy and uses a wheelchair. She is a fifth-year senior at her high school, finishing up a few classes that she could not take last year. Finally, Angie is a fifteen-year-old with cerebral palsy. Reared by her uncle after she was removed from her parents' home by Child Protective Services, she has a busy life that includes playing on several adaptive sports teams, dating, and writing poetry.

But while their individual circumstances differ, each of the stories reveals a young person who is unwilling to be a passive observer in his or her environment. Their stories illustrate the frustrations and irritation they feel at some aspects of life, while still looking hopefully at their futures as young men and women in an able-bodied world.

Dennis

"ONE THING I'VE LEARNED, MAYBE
MORE THAN OTHER KIDS, IS TO
TAKE ONE DAY AT A TIME. I CAN'T
THINK ABOUT BEING SICK OR
BEING DISABLED OR WHATEVER."

I drive slowly past the houses on the north side of the city, hoping to spot an address. Few have numbers visible; several houses have windows and doors boarded up. Once a thriving residential area, this neighborhood has become a refuge for low-income families, too poor or too uninterested to keep the house painted or the grass mowed.

Groups of teenage boys in gang colors stand in the street near a rusted-out Buick. Across the street, a man stands on his front porch, waving frantically. This is Dennis's house, and Don, his father, has been keeping watch for me, making sure I arrive safely.

AN EXCITING NEIGHBORHOOD

Don is a perpetual smiler, with a wiry build and a shock of black hair. He talks fast as he welcomes me through the front door. "I'm glad you found the place okay," he says, shaking my hand. "It's a little tricky, with the circle you have to go around and double back. I was kind of keeping my eye out, you know.

"This isn't the greatest area nowadays," he says with a grin. "I've lived here all my life, right here in this neighborhood. Went to the neighborhood grade school, to North High School right here. But it's changed a lot. It can be, I guess you'd have to say, an exciting neighborhood. But not in a good way, you know?"

The first floor of the house is homey, with a living room centered around a large television. Newspapers and books crowd the tables.

Walking slowly through the darkened kitchen toward the living room is a teenage boy. He moves stiffly and smiles uncertainly, as though he is used to being watched by strangers. Don sees him and smiles again. One doesn't have to be in this house more than a few minutes to realize this father and son are very close.

"Come on, Dennis, come on in here," he says encouragingly. "This is my son Dennis," he says proudly, motioning to the teen. "He's a great kid."

"HE HAD A LOT OF PROBLEMS"

Dennis shakes hands and sits at the table next to his father. He smiles again, a little more confidently and begins. "I'm fifteen," he says, stammering a little. "I'm a freshman at North High,

Dennis, who has a multitude of health problems, including asthma and a heart condition, has endured twelve different surgeries and has spent more than six hundred days of his life in the hospital.

not too far from here. And I guess if you'd talked to the doctors when I was born, they'd probably say that was impossible—me living this long, huh, Dad?"

His father grins. "Yeah, they didn't give Dennis much of a chance, that's for sure. He's had a lot of problems, lots of health problems since the day he was born. One eye that's blind, heart problems when he was born—congestive heart failure, they called that. He has always had asthma pretty bad."

Dennis listens quietly. "I also had to have a head shunt put in when I was a baby," he adds. "That's like a tube that runs from the top of my head down my body into my stomach. That's because I was hydrocephalic. It means that I had pressure on my brain, and they had to relieve it."

Don nods. "See, like in a normal situation, like for you and me, there are vents that drain off fluid from our brains," he explains, pointing behind Dennis's neck. "When that fluid drains off, it relieves that pressure or whatever. But Dennis didn't have that, so they had to give him a shunt.

"See here?" he says, touching a spot behind Dennis's left ear. "He's got a shunt still, always will. It's just under the skin there; you can't see it real good, but if Dennis took his shirt off, you could see it further down going to his stomach."

"OVER SIX HUNDRED DAYS IN THE HOSPITAL"

"Anyway," Don says, "Dennis here sure paid his dues early. He's had twelve different surgeries, and has been over six hundred days in the hospital! More than your share of that stuff. Right, Dennis?"

Dennis grins. "Yeah, and for lots of it, I was too little to remember. I know I was a premature baby; I was born like six weeks early or so. I weighed three pounds—that's like nothing! Before I was born, the doctors didn't have any reason to think I wouldn't be healthy, just like any other little baby. My mom had already had another baby (not with my dad, by another father). So it wasn't like I was at risk or anything.

"They found all this stuff out when I was born. My mom had a C–section, a cesarean. My dad wasn't in the delivery room, were you, Dad?"

"Nah," says Don, shaking his head. "Back in those days, they didn't let the dads in for C–sections. Maybe they thought it was too bloody for us guys. Only in regular deliveries. But hey, bloody stuff doesn't bother me! I'm a Vietnam vet, and I've seen more than my share. Anyway, I got plenty of experience with that blood-and-guts stuff *after* you came home from the hospital!"

"You Were Somewhere Between Green and Blue"

Dennis says that the doctors were not optimistic about his chances of living with so many things wrong with him.

"They told my mom and dad to take me home and have me baptized—and come back soon for the surgeries," he says. "My dad has told me about that. They figured my parents wanted me baptized, just in case, you know?"

Besides putting in a head shunt, doctors knew that Dennis's heart problems needed to be addressed quickly.

"He was a pretty green-looking baby," says Don, chuckling. "You were, Dennis; you were somewhere between green and blue. Your problem was something called a patent ductus. The way it was explained to me is this duct is open when the baby is still inside the mother because it lets the mother's blood flow into the fetus.

"But it's supposed to close off after the baby's born, it's supposed to happen automatically. Now, with Dennis, that duct didn't close, so they had to surgically close it. I guess nowadays that isn't as big a deal—doctors do it regularly. But fifteen years ago, it was touch and go. It was really scary."

Adventures with the Feeding Tube

So scary, says Don, that baby Dennis was unable to nurse or drink from a bottle like a normal baby. Because he was so premature and his body underdeveloped, he had to be fed by means of a feeding tube.

"That was no easy thing," remembers Don. "That went on eighteen months: getting that tube in his tummy, using a syringe to get the thing going. And sometimes Dennis—you know how babies just jerk around with their hands and feet—he'd sometimes make the process even harder because he'd yank that tube right out! The whole tube would go flinging across the room!"

Dennis laughs, clearly enjoying this account of his infant misbehavior.

"My dad had to keep taking me back to the emergency room when I'd do that, so they could reattach the tube," he says. "He's

Dennis and his father, Don, share a playful moment. Don decided when Dennis was a baby that he would care for him in his home instead of placing him in an institution.

told me about this. And finally, after one time, he just told the doctors to show him how to do it so he didn't have to keep coming back to the hospital when I'd yank it out."

Don nods. "Like I said before, I'd been in Nam, I wasn't too bothered by the blood and stuff. I could handle that, I mean, it's my little boy. How could I not do that for him? And it sure was easier to reattach a tube in his stomach at home than bundle him up and get him to the hospital all the time, you know?"

"SHE JUST COULDN'T HANDLE IT, I GUESS"

But while Don was able to adjust to the demands of having a severely disabled child, his wife was not. When Dennis was six months old, she left the family, never to return.

"It's hard to say why it happened," says Don sadly. "She just couldn't handle it, I guess. Didn't like that gory stuff. I'm not painting her to be evil or anything. But we had a strong difference of opinion on how to deal with our son. She favored putting him in a home where he would be taken care of. I wanted him to stay with us.

"See, when Dennis was born, and as it became clear that he was going to have a tougher go of it than most kids, the doctors were giving us options. I mean, they didn't know, really. I think this about doctors—they try. They give you all the information they know, but they can't really tell you the answers."

"THEY DON'T KNOW EVERYTHING"

"But they don't know everything. There were so many things about Dennis they didn't know; they didn't even know from one week to the next if he was going to survive! With all the brain problems, with the heart problems, no one could say if he was going to even grow up, or to live to his next birthday. How much damage had been done? Who knew?

"They told us how he might not grow much physically, like he might be a little tiny midget. But they didn't know, and clearly, that isn't the case. They wanted us to learn sign language when he was little, because they didn't even know if he would learn to talk, or walk, or anything. You just had to go one day at a time, just riding with it, you know?"

Don says that when doctors gave them the option of placing Dennis in a more institutional setting, his wife agreed. "It wasn't like the doctors were suggesting it—they were just showing us options," he recalls. "They weren't taking sides. It was more like, 'If you can do it, do it.' And I wanted to do it. And his mother—well, she couldn't do it. Maybe it bothered her seeing the gruesome stuff, I don't know. Too much stress, too many doctors, too many crises all the time.

"Anyway, it became with us, 'Put him in an institution, or I'm out of here.' And I couldn't do it. I just couldn't think about this little life we'd created, about leaving him. So we broke up. She's in Chicago now; she doesn't come around. Once in awhile she'll call, but not often. It's sad for Dennis, I know that."

"I DON'T REMEMBER THAT FAR BACK"

Dennis says that his early memories are mostly of hospitals. "I know the first two years of my life, that was pretty much where I lived," he says, smiling. "I was back and forth between two different hospitals, depending on what surgery I was having. I don't remember that far back, but I know just from my dad telling me.

"There were a lot of life-threatening times, I guess. My dad told me it was like one emergency after another—that after awhile it truly got to the point where the word 'emergency' didn't sound like an emergency any more. Just normal!

"I remember one time, I was in the hospital for something—I don't remember what. I think I was about six or seven. I remember I was watching a Big Bird video with my dad, and I had a seizure. I don't remember the seizure, but I remember hearing about it."

Don shudders. "Boy, that's for sure," he says, shaking his head. "He was in there because he had a hole in his heart—and he got the wrong medicine, I think, and had a reaction or something. It was one of the scariest times. Anyway, the emergency staff came running in and brought out this huge, huge needle," he says, widening his hands eighteen inches apart, "and gave him a shot right into his heart. Then he was in a coma for a day. We didn't know then if he was going to come out of it."

HARD TO MAKE FRIENDS

While Dennis's medical problems and complications made life difficult, he says that they affected more than just his physical well-being.

"I think being in and out of hospitals like I was made it hard socially, too," he admits. "I mean, for awhile I was in sign language school, then I was in regular school. And then I missed school all the time because I was sick or because I had another operation or something. It was great having my dad be there every time, but I kind of missed having friends like all the other kids had.

"Sometimes I'd miss like two weeks of school, and I'd come back and I felt like I'd been gone a year. Everybody just seemed to be doing stuff I didn't do. I'd try to make friends, and sometimes I did. I'd start talking to a kid, and we'd get to be friends, and just when I was comfortable, it seemed like something would happen and I'd be back in the hospital for another two or three weeks!"

Dennis says that because of his disability, he looked and moved differently from the other kids.

"I know they looked at me and wondered what was the matter with me," he says. "They didn't understand me or what I'd been through. They didn't really understand why I was always gone, always missing school. So that was hard."

Dennis plays basketball with a neighborhood friend. Because of Dennis's disabilities, making friends has not always been easy.

"OUR OWN TIMETABLE"

Don has been listening intently to his son, and he nods sympathetically.

"You know, we were just sort of off on our own," he says, shrugging. "We had our own timetable for doing things; you couldn't go by what normal families did, or when they accomplished things.

"Take potty training, for example. I mean, I think Dennis was like seven years old before he was completely trained. It seemed like when he was a toddler, we'd get real close, and then, boom! He'd be back in the hospital, and they'd put him in diapers again. So that was rough on us, rough on Dennis, who wanted to feel like he was getting to be a big boy, but still not trained yet, you know?

"I know it was hard on him as a little kid. He missed out on a lot. But man, he was so tiny, so helpless a lot of the time. He stayed small for so long, and he would get so sick—just a cold would knock him for a loop. The look on his face, man, it was scary watching him try to breathe! He was a brave kid, braver than lots of adults would be when he'd have to have all those tests, all that blood work and everything. Really patient, really tough. I admired him—still do."

"MONEY WAS TIGHT"

One hardship Dennis and Don have both had to deal with is the lack of money. Medical care—especially the amount Dennis needs—is extremely expensive.

"I was a parole officer for over eight years before Dennis came along," says Don. "But there was no way I could keep doing that and take care of him. It's not like with a normal, healthy kid, you can put him in day care pretty early on. Dennis needed round-the-clock care, and there was no way that I could expect a day care provider to do all that stuff with the feeding tube. I don't think I could have even found one who'd be willing to try!

"I ended up quitting my job and going on, well, welfare," he says quietly. "I'm not proud of that, but what do you do? You hear

Dennis's father speaks proudly of his son and recalls Dennis's bravery and patience in dealing with constant medical problems. "I admired him—still do," he says.

about some people saying how they can't afford to work, and that was us! If I worked, I'd be spending every penny trying to get full nursing care for Dennis.

"So I quit being a parole officer. The state took care of the medical bills—most of them, anyway. And boy, things were expensive! Dennis had three heart surgeries in a row, and that came out to a little more than five hundred thousand dollars! But with welfare, we had a real limited income—even though the insurance part was good. I remember for awhile, our check every month was just barely enough for rent, food, and transportation. We had no money to save, or any left over for anything.

"When Dennis was little, his asthma was really giving him trouble, especially in the summer. We really needed an air conditioner; the doctors said it would help a lot, but the insurance wouldn't pay for it. That's when you get to know the agencies around the city, places that can help you cut through the red tape. We went to a community emergency agency that helped us. You don't think about places like that, and the good work that they do, until you find yourself in the position of needing them!" says Don.

LOTS OF SUPPORT

As Dennis grew and was able to be in school most of the time, Don was able to go back to work.

"I'm working part-time as a maintenance man at my brother's computer place," he says. "It's been a lifesaving job; my brother has been so great, letting me choose my hours so I can be there for Dennis when I need to be. That's when you know how great your family is.

"I've got a great family. They've been behind me through all of it—financially, giving me rides to the hospital when I didn't have a car, you name it. When times were rough, they'd help out. My sister would come over with food sometimes. My brother would lend me money when I needed it. We even get to go up to my brother's cabin up north sometimes. You can't know how much they mean to us. Right, Dennis?"

Dennis nods emphatically. "They're great. I hear kids say sometimes how they can't stand being around all their uncles and aunts, like for holidays and stuff. I figure I'm really lucky; I can't imagine not having them around."

"We Can Deal with Pretty Much Everything"

Dennis says that while he still has a number of medical problems, he is far better off today than he was ten or twelve years ago.

"I've got one eye that doesn't see," he says. "And my one leg is more developed than the other one, and shorter, too. So I guess I can't walk or run exactly the same as everyone else. I don't run fast, but I try. My heart defect is taken care of now, so that isn't a big thing.

"But the biggest problem now is asthma, I guess. That's the thing that gets in the way most of the time. We have a nebulizer—that's like a mask I wear for awhile, with real moist air that I breathe. That helps my lungs when it's hard to get enough air in. I do about three nebulizer treatments each day. Usually that helps, but once in awhile, I have to go into the hospital. Not as often as I used to—before my immune system got stronger. But once in awhile it's really hard to breathe and the nebulizer just doesn't do it.

"Last summer we were fighting this bladder problem—I had blood in my urine, you know? It's like I was thinking, 'Man, where do all these things come from?' I don't know anyone who had that before! But we dealt with it, and it hasn't happened since. I figure my dad and I have been through a lot worse stuff, and we can deal with pretty much everything."

"I Love School"

Dennis says that he has a lot of things he's enjoying in his life right now, including school.

"I love school," he says with a smile. "I'm a good student, too."

Don jumps up and grabs something from the top of his desk.

"Look at this," he says proudly, displaying a certificate from North High School with Dennis's name emblazoned upon it. "This is how good a student he is—honor roll! Boy, those doctors fifteen years ago wouldn't have believed this at all! This is from last semester, and I'll bet he can do it again. Right, Dennis?"

Dennis shrugs, visibly pleased. "I hope. I like the kids at the school, and everybody pretty much treats me fine. I'm not as bad off as some of the disabled kids there; I feel really lucky. I'd hate to not be active, to not move around. I'd get bored, antsy to go outside and do something.

Even with his multiple disabilities, Dennis tries to remain active. "I'd hate to . . . get bored, antsy to go outside and do something."

"I had a good background at St. Elizabeth Seton School before I started high school. I was in a public junior high before that, but I didn't stay there too long."

He looks at his father.

"Dennis doesn't have problems with kids now, but back then a couple years ago, it was hard," Don explains, looking down at his hands. "The other kids, well, kids can be cruel. Everybody knows that. Some kids, they kind of have a knack of picking out the weak ones, and they go after them, you know?

"Anyway, Dennis was one of the only ones, and they made his life miserable for a while. They'd steal his money, take his lunch, just be mean. He'd hide out in the computer room so he wouldn't have to face them. As soon as I heard about that, I got him out of there—and St. Elizabeth Seton's was great. No problems."

"Kids Are Great Now"

Now, at fifteen, Dennis claims that life is generally pretty good, even with his disabilities. He has no trouble making friends; in fact, he says, his father would say that it is quite the opposite.

The kids at Dennis's new school are more tolerant of disabled kids than they were at his old school. "I like the kids at the school," he says, "and everybody pretty much treats me fine."

"My dad is always telling me to get off the phone," he says with a smile. "I like to talk—that's just how it is. I've got friends from school, and my best friend, Aaron. He lives just like a block away; we've been best friends since sixth grade, I guess."

What do he and Aaron like to do?

Dennis shrugs. "We do lots of stuff," he says. "We play sports, watch TV, stuff like that."

"And talk to girls," Don reminds him.

"Yeah, and talk to girls," says Dennis, refusing to rise to the bait. "That's what I like to do. I have a girlfriend, sort of. I mean, we're really close friends, so we're mostly that, I guess. She's great, though. Her name's Vanessa, and she's lots of fun to be around. And her friend Kelly is nice, too. They're both coming over here Friday night, just to hang around, listen to music, whatever."

Are the kids at his high school more tolerant of disabled kids than his first junior high?

Dennis nods. "Yeah, no question," he says. "I mean, I really wanted to go to North. Aaron and my other friends were going there, and I wanted to go to the same school with them. My dad said we'd give it a try, but if the kids started, you know, eating me up over there, being mean or whatever, we'd go to a different place. But it's been fine; the kids are great now."

"HE WANTS ME TO BE OUT THERE AS MUCH AS I CAN"

Dennis says that with his multiple disabilities, he could be getting more specialized treatment, but he doesn't want it.

"My dad and I talked about it," he says. "He and I kind of think the same thing: he wants me to be out there as much as I can, you know, be out with the other kids. And if I can't always keep up, at least I'm trying.

"I could be taking a special bus to school, with other disabled kids, but I don't want to. I have nothing against them at all, but I want to try to be as much like the regular kids as I can. I guess that's the best way to say it. I'd rather try hard with them than be the top one among the disabled kids.

"I have a note from a doctor that lists all the stuff I've had, the congestive heart failure, the head shunt, the asthma, whatever. And I could use it to get out of lots of stuff, like regular phys ed, I guess. But I don't want to. I'll keep the letter, in case something comes up and I really need special help. But so far, I'm doing okay—and as you can tell, the letter is just sitting here! I'm not using it.

"Man," he says, grinning at his father, "I know some kids that would *pay* to have a note like that!"

Don rolls his eyes.

LIMITS

But while his disabilities are not so severe that he needs special treatment at school, Dennis acknowledges that there are limits in the things he can do.

"I love sports," he begins. "I love watching, but I love playing even more. My dad set up a basketball hoop in our backyard, and the two of us play back there, or Aaron and I play."

Is he any good?

Dennis smiles shyly. "I don't know—I can't run so great. That's because of the difference in my legs. And sometimes my asthma gets bad. But I try my hardest every time. That's important to me, to always try," he says.

Don says that it's important for Dennis to learn to pace himself, and while he is getting better at it, he still needs to pay attention to his body.

While Dennis enjoys watching sports, he likes playing sports even more. He admits, though, that there are limits to the things he can do. For instance, his asthma sometimes hinders him but, he says, "I try my hardest every time."

"Dennis tries to be too much of a tough guy, especially when he's playing basketball or something," Don says. "I have to remind him to stop if he's breathing hard—we both know what can happen if he doesn't pay attention to that. But it's hard to tell him no. There are some things you just don't want to deny a kid, you know?

"Like when he was younger, one of his doctors told me not to let him go into the swimming pool. He got earaches, you know, and that could turn into more serious complications for Dennis. But man, how do you tell a kid when it's summertime, ninety-five degrees out, that he can't go swimming? So he goes, but he just has to be real careful not to get water in his ears, I guess."

LITTLE THINGS CAN BECOME BIG THINGS

Dennis is acutely aware that little health problems can quickly become scary ones if he isn't careful.

"I stay inside a lot in the winter," he says. "That's my least favorite time of the year. If I didn't have problems, I would be out doing stuff, but it seems like there's so many germs going around in the winter, so many people with strep throat, or colds, or whatever.

"And for a regular kid, it's no big deal. But if I get a bad cold, it can get complicated with breathing problems, because of my asthma, you know? So I stay in, I play computer, stuff like that."

Does he play on any sports teams at school?

He shakes his head. "No, I wouldn't survive," he admits. "The kids are too fast. I can hold my own with my dad, and my friends, just playing for fun. But I'd never be able to compete with those other guys. There are adapted sports at my school, but I don't do those."

Don nods. "He's been asked to come out to Courage Center [an organization for the handicapped], where they have leagues and stuff for kids with disabilites. But he doesn't want to go. He always says he'd rather do his best and be with the regular kids. Maybe sometime he'll change his mind."

PCA

Another part of his life that Dennis enjoys is the time with his personal care attendant or PCA.

"Her name is Barb," he explains, "and I stay with her every other weekend. She lives north of here about forty-five minutes away in a great house! She's got a pool, all kinds of sports stuff like volleyball and basketball.

"It gives me a break from being home all the time, and my dad a break, too. It isn't as intense as it used to be all the time when I was always sick, but it's still nice for my dad to get a little time to himself. Anyway, for the last six years, Barb has been my PCA.

"She makes sure I do my homework, supervises me. And if a medical thing comes up, she knows exactly what to do, so my dad doesn't have to worry. She's got the nebulizer and everything, too. She teaches me stuff, too, like cooking and stuff I need to be on my own someday."

NO PETS

One thing Dennis says would make the time pass more quickly on winter days spent indoors would be a pet. Unfortunately, he says, that's one thing his asthma just won't allow.

"It seems like no matter what kind—dog, cat, hamster, whatever—I have breathing problems around them," he says. "I love animals, always have. And I was hoping to get a job on weekends at this one pet store, but it won't work for me, I guess."

Noticing a large empty aquarium behind him in the dining room, I ask if he'd tried fish.

He shoots a quick look at his father and they both smile sadly. "Yeah, we had some once," says Don. "It's not the greatest kind of pet, not one you can get close to though. Right, Dennis? And we did have a couple of real pretty sunfish in there one time. A friend caught them and brought them over, and we put them in there.

"They lasted a long time, though, like eight months. But they're real dirty fish, and you have to wash out the aquarium really often. That was the trouble, and we had a sort of accident."

Dennis explains, "My dad sort of fried them, without meaning to. See, you have to get the hose from the basement, and he went downstairs to turn the water on, and he put in hot instead of cold. He didn't catch it in time, and they died. We both felt really bad about that."

Don sighs. "I know he'd be less lonesome with a pet, but I gotta look at it this way—he hasn't been sick ever since we've been without pets. Right, Dennis? I mean, that's the way we like it, you not having to go to the emergency room for a breathing treatment. I guess we'll learn to live without the pets."

Dennis plays with a friend's cat. Though he would love to have a cat of his own, his breathing problems prohibit him from having any pets other than fish.

LOOKING AHEAD

Ask him about what kind of plans he has for the future, and Dennis admits he is unsure.

"I sometimes think I have—what do you call it? Déjà vu," he announces.

His father brightens. "Do we win the lottery?" he asks. "Should I buy a ticket?"

"No," Dennis says, laughing. "I mean, I feel like I've done things before, sometimes. Like I can imagine how it would feel. I think about jobs, and I can almost imagine what it would be like. I sometimes think it would be cool to be a doctor, or maybe someone else who helps people.

"I don't want to make up my mind yet, though, because I'll just change it before too long anyway. I know one thing: I have to keep

Dennis longs for the day when he'll have more independence but, he says, "I'll always be buddies with my dad."

doing good in school. If I do, I'll have more choices of things I can do later on. Having choices is really important."

For now, Dennis says, the only future he really allows himself to think seriously about is the not-too-distant one.

"I think about maybe getting my license," he says, smiling. "I am like legally blind in one eye, but I'm good in the other one. And I will be able to drive at some point. So I think about that, and about going to dances in school and stuff. Getting a job—although my dad isn't real big on that."

"I told him he'll be working all his life," says Don. "I want him to enjoy being a kid—it sure doesn't last long. And he got kind of gypped out of his childhood, with all the health problems he's had."

"Being on My Own"

But Dennis seems eager to get on with his life. He's impatient, and he admits it. "I know my life will change when I work, or when I can drive a car," he says. "It will be really nice, too. Being more in-dependent, making my own choices, being on my own sometimes. Believe me, that's one thing you don't get to be when you're sick all the time. You get so used to doctors and nurses—I feel like I'm a regular at the hospital!

"One thing I've learned, maybe more than other kids, is to take one day at a time. I can't think about being sick or being disabled or whatever—that it's my whole life. I just say, 'I have a cough to-day,' or 'I feel sick tonight.' I just learn to work with how I feel, and I deal with that."

He smiles again, without embarrassment. "And I know, no mat-ter how old I get, or how independent I am, I'll always be buddies with my dad. We've really been through a lot."

Patrick

"I USED TO THINK THAT I WAS THE
ONLY ONE IN MY CLASS AT SCHOOL
WHO HAD PROBLEMS. . . . BUT I
KNOW THAT ISN'T TRUE."

The living room is cheerful and cozy; roadrunner and desert scenes give it a Southwestern look. Patrick's mother laughs, acknowledging the large number of cactus figures adorning the shelves.

"I'm from California," Carol says. "I miss the desert—so this is the result."

Her son Patrick, age thirteen, comes into the room behind her. He is Asian, a nice-looking boy with wire-rimmed glasses and a shy smile. He walks stiffly, and his hands appear twisted. To a casual observer, it seems that Patrick has cerebral palsy, but Patrick says no.

"I HAVE ARTHROGRYPOSIS"

"I have arthrogryposis," he says, pronouncing each syllable distinctly. "It's something I was born with, but I'm not sure why."

He looks at Carol, who explains. "Arthrogryposis is a mouthful, but it's only part of the name," she says. "The full name is arthrogryposis multiplex congenita, or AMC for short. And, as Patrick says, it's a birth defect. It can be genetic sometimes; other times not.

"Pat's is not, so there is no concern for him about passing the condition on. Most cases that aren't genetic are caused by some kind of fetal crowding in the uterus. For instance, if the baby grows fast and the uterus is small and doesn't keep up, that can cause crowding.

"Other times, it may involve twins. The more active one takes up more of the room as they are developing. The fetus that is crowded ends up with joints that don't move. Instead, they contract, get less flexible. Muscles don't develop as they're meant to, so there is missing or misformed muscle tissue."

"It Doesn't Hurt"

Pat says that other kids in his school have wondered about what is wrong with his hands, and why he doesn't walk the same as they do.

"One time a kid in school asked me if my hands hurt, because of how they are," he says, looking down. "But it doesn't hurt. I told him that. It just feels regular; it just is how I am. And I'm pretty used to how I am. It isn't any worse now than when I was born. The doctors must have known right away that I had it—that was back in Korea, before I came here on the airplane."

Pat smiles and says that his is a good family to be in because two of his siblings also have AMC.

"My big sister Em has it; she's sixteen. And my younger sister Rachel does, too; she's nine," he says. "My big brother Ben doesn't have that. But we're all Korean; my parents adopted all of us. I guess they must have wanted Korean children!"

"We'd Never Even Heard of AMC"

Carol agrees with Patrick's assessment. She says that when she and her husband Jonathan were ready to be parents, they didn't start off thinking that they would adopt children with special needs.

"When we started adopting, the agency gave us a list of special needs, special conditions," she remembers. "And they asked us to check ones that we might consider. Well, we'd never even heard of AMC then. One of the things we did check was cleft lip—and our first child, Ben, had bilateral [both sides] cleft lip and gum.

"When we went for our second adoption, we got a referral for a little girl who had arthrogryposis. We didn't know anything about that. We just wanted to be parents, as I said. That's all we knew. Anyway, with Em, we learned all we could about the condition—we had our family doctor to help us, and we lined up everyone beforehand that we'd need for her care.

"And when we decided to adopt another child, we decided that special needs were okay, as long as it was one we were already familiar with—either cleft lip or arthrogryposis. We had the routine down for those, and we felt like we could handle either one. And we got Patrick."

Patrick was born with arthrogryposis, a birth defect that prevents muscles from developing normally and requires him to wear leg braces.

COMING FROM KOREA

Patrick has heard these stories before, and enjoys them. "I was eleven months old when I came from Korea," he says. "My mom and dad knew that my arthrogryposis was worse than Em's. But it wasn't as bad as they first thought. When they had sent a report from Korea referring me, they said that I might not have any use of my arms at all!"

Carol nods. "However, one of the pictures they sent us showed Patrick lying on his back in a crib, with his arms lifted up playing with a toy! Clearly, he could use his arms to some extent.

"He had club feet—severely club feet," she says. "They turned completely inward toward each other. His hands were bent at the wrist, and turned outward. When Patrick arrived, his thumbs were pulled way into the palms of his hands."

Pat adds, "But today I'm better. I've had leg operations, and my left leg can bend even farther than my right; it's the best one. I had an operation when I was in kindergarten and had to miss a lot of school. When I came back, I had to have a cast on and be in a wheelchair for awhile. Later on, I had a cast shoe, so I could walk around with my cast. I remember that, too; it was so heavy."

Carol says that his thumbs are quite a bit better than they were when he was an infant, too. She attributes the improvement to an unlikely source.

"Video games," she says. "I think Nintendo has been great therapy. It's done more for Patrick, in our opinion, than some sort of standard exercises or physical therapy. And far more enjoyable, I'm sure!"

SURGERIES

Pat's first surgeries occurred very soon after coming to his adopted family. "I think I was like fifteen or sixteen months old," he says,

Patrick's mother believes that playing video games has helped Patrick to improve the use of his thumbs. "I think Nintendo has been great therapy," she says.

looking at his mother for confirmation. "I had one and then after two weeks I had another one. My right hip wasn't in its socket—I think that's pretty common for a person with arthrogryposis. Then the next surgery was for my clubfeet. I had to be in a full body cast, from my chest down to my toes, for six weeks—not easy when you're a baby!

"But my parents say I was really a good baby, and didn't fuss and cry too much. That surprised them, I guess. Mom says that my brother and sister distracted me and played with me so I forgot about crying."

Carol nods. "That's true. We have pictures of him from that time in his body cast, laughing and smiling. He was the easiest baby I can ever imagine! With all that discomfort and everything, he'd certainly have had good cause to be fussy."

MORE POSSIBILITIES?

Are there more operations in his future?

Patrick says he doesn't think so. "I know there isn't a way to cure my disability," he says slowly. "There isn't like an operation that will make it go away. I haven't had any operations on my hands or on my arms, and I don't know if they can do anything about how mine are."

Carol says that doctors now do surgeries to straighten hands—surgery that wasn't an option when Patrick was a baby. However, she maintains, there is a trade-off.

"There's a very respected local surgeon who does this," she says. "He'll put the hands in what they call 'neutral position,' so the hand is not bent down, but straight. But see, then the hand is locked in that position. It's not as though he would have flexibility.

"We might have considered it if it had been an option when Patrick was little. But once he started to learn adaptations—ways he could cope with his hands in that position—we'd just be setting him back. He would have to relearn everything he'd already learned.

"For instance, video games would no longer be an option for him if his hands were surgically changed. So you're really ex-changing one set of disabilities for another with the surgery. Your hands *look* more normal, and that can be a consideration. If, when he gets older, he decides that he wants to make that trade-off—and we're convinced he understands all the aspects of it—then we'll look into it."

"We Made a Decision Early On"

With four children, three of whom have arthrogryposis, Carol says that she and her husband had to think about how much surgery would be involved in their lives.

"We made a decision early on," she says, choosing her words carefully, "when the kids were very young. We decided that they weren't going to spend their childhood as patients. Surgery that could fix something or give them more mobility—that's one thing.

"But something purely for cosmetic reasons or something of that sort, no. We felt it was important that our kids not spend most of their time in hospitals or recovering from surgeries. I'm not criticizing parents who decide otherwise—but for us, this seemed like the best route to take."

Patrick agrees. "I didn't like the times I had to have the surgery. I don't remember the ones when I was a baby, but I remember the one in kindergarten. I didn't like missing school, and I didn't like having the wheelchair after I came back. When you have operations, you miss a lot."

"I Didn't Used to Think About Fair and Unfair"

Patrick says that he understands there are differences between him and classmates but insists that most people who know him don't treat him any differently than they do others.

"I think they usually treat me the same," he says. "I like being a regular person in my class. I know I walk different, but I think people don't think about that when they're with me. I don't think I knew I was different until I was in kindergarten, when I had to be in the wheelchair. Then I noticed that I wasn't the same as the other kids.

"I don't like to stand out. Sometimes in gym class, I can't do the same things the other kids do. Like if they're playing a game or something that I wouldn't be able to play because of my hands, or because of how I walk. And then, sitting and watching on the sidelines, I feel kind of lonesome sometimes. But sometimes other people sit out, too—like if they get hurt, or are being bad or something—then there's someone to talk to.

"And there are plenty of other times when I *can* play the game. Like when they're doing strength training, or exercises like that. I can do push-ups and curl-ups—modified ones. I'm pretty good at those. I try most things, and I'm not too bad."

He thinks a minute. "There's one game that's really hard, though—shuffle-puck-run. I have trouble picking up the puck from the floor, for some reason. It's kind of a flat shape, and it's hard for me to get a grip on it. But usually I do okay in most of the other stuff."

Does he feel that life has been unfair to him?

Patrick takes a minute to consider his answer. "I didn't used to think about fair and unfair," he says. "Not at all. Sometimes I think that now, but usually it's when I'm in a bad mood about something else. I'm lucky in lots of ways, so I can't say my life has treated me bad."

SCHOOL

Patrick admits that school ranks fairly low on the list of things he likes. "Mostly, I don't like it," he says honestly. "If I had a choice, I'd rather have more Saturdays and Sundays. I hate getting up early, I hate all the work—especially the homework and projects the teachers assign. Right now me and my friend Gannon are working on a project for History Day. It's about Pearl Harbor. Gannon's nice, and it's more fun working with a friend, but still—the work! I'd rather be home, watching television.

Patrick and his friend Gannon display their Pearl Harbor project during their school's History Day.

"I guess there are a couple of things I like about school," he continues. "I like gym, lunch, and social studies. And I like going outside after lunch. But that's about it.

"On school days, we have a routine in the morning. My sister Rachel and I get up and have breakfast at the same time; we go to the same school, so we have the same schedule. I usually have a bagel or some cereal and watch *Pokémon*, and then my dad drives us.

"I have a key for the elevator at school. My classes are all on the second floor; Rachel's are on the first floor, so she doesn't use the elevator. I *could* do stairs—I mean, I do them here at home all the time. But the stairs at school, with so many kids going up and down at the same time—I could fall. No one would mean to push or be rough, but it just happens sometimes. So it's safer to take the elevator."

FRIENDS

Patrick says that he has one main friend at school, Gannon. However, he has several other friends in his neighborhood he enjoys hanging around with.

"My best friend is Jerry, though," he says. "He used to go to school with me. I've known him since kindergarten. But then he moved to California, and I didn't see him for a really long time.

"But Jerry recently moved back, and I was really glad. Now he goes to a different school, but he's making plans to transfer back to our old school, where I am now. He'll be coming back this spring, or else in the fall, at the beginning of eighth grade. We haven't seen each other much, but we talk on the phone all the time."

Most days, Patrick says, he comes home from school and just relaxes by himself. "I watch TV, or I play video games," he says. "It might seem hard to believe I can operate the controller, but I'm pretty good at it. My favorite is *Super Smash Brothers*, or maybe *Blitz*—that one's a football game. But I'm saving my money for *Pokémon Stadium*. That's the one I really want."

"WOULD I LOVE TO WIN A MILLION DOLLARS!"

Cartoons—especially ones about superheroes—are still his favorite television shows, although Patrick has lately become a fan of *Who Wants to Be a Millionaire*.

"I don't mean that I get all the questions right," he explains. "I almost always get the first ones, the easy ones. But once in a while

I get an upper-level question right. Boy, would I love to win a million dollars!

"I'd probably buy sports cars," he says, smiling. "Maybe a Ferrari or a Corvette or something. Blue or black—but really, really shiny. And I'd hire some engineers or some people to figure out a way I could drive them—that's possible, I'm sure. I mean, almost *anything* is possible when you're talking about having a million dollars. That would be really great.

"I'd also use the money for trips for our family. I've been to Orlando, to Disney World. And I went to Iowa. Those two places. Our family used to go to Duluth, and that was fun. But we don't go anymore, and I'm not really sure why. But if I had a lot of money, we could go lots of places—our whole family. That's how I like it—when we all go."

More realistically, Patrick says that he enjoys less exciting things than Disney World. "I don't really do sports after school, or anything

Most days after school, Patrick relaxes by playing video games or adding to his Pez collection. He also fits in time for exercise, which prevents the contractures in his muscles from worsening.

like that," he says. "But I walk around my house, and sometimes I watch my big brother and his friends play basketball or football. Ben is really good! I wish I could play, too, sometimes."

Patrick considers this a minute then shakes his head. "But I don't like to spend too much time thinking about that. That kind of thinking just gets you sad, I guess."

His mother nods. "We're glad Patrick does get the exercise he does—even if it isn't organized soccer or baseball like other kids sometimes play. Especially for a person with arthrogryposis, it's good to be active. You don't want the contractures in the muscles to get any worse.

"That doesn't mean that exercise or physical rehabilitation will reverse his condition—it won't. But just like with any other person, if you don't get exercise, you tend to get stiff in your joints. And for people who already have contractures, that just makes it that much worse."

"Getting Help"

Patrick says that in his case, having AMC means that he depends on other people for help in things other kids take for granted.

"I usually don't mind getting help if I need it," he says matter-of-factly. "Like, I need help from my parents getting dressed. I need help putting my leg braces on. See," he says, pulling the bottom of his sweatpants up, "I have these two braces. And they come up to here, right below my knees.

"I wear sweatpants and stuff, things that are easy to pull on and off. I'm used to getting help; that's just the way it is. On weekends, I do it myself—most of it, anyway. That's because I'm not so rushed. I can't get dressed fast, so it's easier to have help. They can do everything so much faster."

One thing that Patrick cannot do, even with the extra time on Saturday or Sunday, is put on his shoes and braces.

"I put on my own socks, then they put on the braces and shoes," he says. "They make sure everything is not too tight and not too loose. The reason I can't do my own shoes is because I can't make a fist. When you are tying, you need to sort of curl your fingers around, all the way in. And I can't do that."

He acknowledges that this is limiting but says that his friends are willing to help if the situation arises. "Like if I sleep over at a friend's house, they'll help me. I don't think they really mind or

41

think about it. It's no big deal to them, which is lucky. I would maybe feel funny asking someone to do these things, I think. But a couple of my friends, they don't even wait for me to ask."

The Hardest Thing

Patrick says there is another situation in which he must rely on other people, one which he worries about a great deal.

"It's falling," he says quietly. "I hate falling. It's the one thing I think about, and it gets me nervous sometimes. Sometimes I even dream about it!

"See, if I fall, I can't get up. Not unless I'm close to a chair, or a table, or something I can hold onto to drag myself up again. It's because my arms are the way they are. See, I can't catch myself if I start to lose my balance. I don't have the strength and the reflexes.

"So if I fell, I could really get hurt, and that's scary. But even more than getting hurt, I worry about falling and being by myself, and lying there. That would be horrible, just lying there, not able to get up. Sometimes I think about that—like being outside by myself and falling. I'd just have to stay like that, not moving, until someone came by and noticed me."

"It Made Me Feel Embarrassed"

Patrick's mother adds that the fear of falling is a very common fear among people with AMC.

"I've talked to adults who have this disability," she says, "and they have the same worry—falling when they are alone. Almost every other situation can be managed; people find ways to work around almost anything. But there are no ways to work around this.

"I think it's especially hard for a boy of Patrick's age. It makes him feel vulnerable in ways that his peers are not. You'd have to see it to understand, I guess. For an absolutely flat surface, without a railing or a curb or something, he would be pretty much stuck—and that's scary for a young person who is at the age when they want to feel more independence."

Patrick has been in such a situation, he says—although not often. "It happened at school a couple of times, and other kids helped me up. I felt two different ways about that," he says, thinking about it. "I felt glad they were there, and I felt funny, too. It kind of made me feel embarrassed, kind of weird. Really, it isn't something I like to even think about."

Patrick admits that, like many other kids, he would rather be watching television than doing his homework.

"EVERYONE MOSTLY GETS ALONG"

Within his secure family environment, Patrick says he feels happy more often than not.

"I get mad at my younger sister, Rachel," he admits. "And that's something I have to work on, I guess. I get irritated with her when she comes into the room when I am doing homework or something, and starts screaming and yelling.

"I love her because she's my sister, but that doesn't mean I don't get mad at her. I should be nicer to her, I guess. I mean, I'm thirteen now, and I should have more patience. I think Ben and Em were probably annoyed with me a lot when I was little, but I don't think they ever got mad like I do.

Younger sister Rachel watches as Patrick plays a game. "I love her because she's my sister," he says. "But that doesn't mean I don't get mad at her."

"Other than that, I think in my family, everyone mostly gets along. My brother and I used to share a room, but when we moved into this house, we got separate ones. That was back when Ben was twelve, I think."

His mother nods. "It isn't that Patrick is messy or that the boys didn't get along. But because of his disability, we can't really use shelves for Patrick's stuff. He can't reach up to get things off them. He has always needed to have things down where he could get them without raising his arms."

CHANGING HIS ROOM

She smiles at her son. "We've always had bins and things down on the floor—for all his cars, toys, all that stuff he played with. That didn't leave much space for Ben in the old days, did it?"

Patrick shakes his head. "Ben's much neater, and he got mad that there wasn't any floor space for his stuff. So when we got our own rooms, it was easier on everybody.

"I still need things lower level now. But I don't have bins around anymore; there's more room on my floor. I just got a computer, and my parents told me that they couldn't fit a computer desk in my room, plus a chair, and still have room for the bins of toys.

"Really," he adds, "I don't play that often with those toys. Once in a while, but now they're in the closet. If I need something, like Hot Wheels or something, I just ask someone to get them down for me. But I have room for the computer, which I really like."

"My Bad Things Are Just Different"

Patrick says that he sometimes gets discouraged or angry because of his disability; however, he doesn't dwell on it.

"I used to think that I was the only one in my class at school who had problems, who thought about bad things," he says. "I thought all the other kids were lucky, because everything was fine for them.

"But I know that isn't true. Now that I'm older, I know better. Everyone has things they are embarrassed about, or that they wish they could change. Some kids do really bad in school, or have mean parents, or parents who don't pay attention to them.

"I don't have those problems. I worry about things like falling or not being able to play in phys ed. But another kid might worry about stuff too. I don't think I have more bad things in my life. They're just different."

"I Usually Ignore Them at First"

Even so, he says, he gets annoyed by things that he can't change. "I don't like to feel different," he says, shrugging. "I don't worry about it, but I sometimes feel bad when I'm the only one sitting out in phys ed, or if they're playing something I can't do at recess. I usually try, but sometimes I'm not good.

"I also hate it when people stare at me. Nobody at school would laugh at me, they've all known me for a long time, and they're not like that anyway. But sometimes like if I'm at the mall, and little kids stare at me because of how I walk or how my hands are, I feel bad.

"I try not to let them see my feelings are hurt. I usually ignore them at first," he confides. "That works sometimes. But sometimes I turn around to see if they're still staring at me. I hope they aren't! Sometimes they're still looking, or they're laughing with their friends, and I feel like they're laughing at me. But sometimes they just forget about me and do something else. That's a relief, when that happens."

"I'm Not Sure What My Limits Will Be"

Patrick says that he doesn't know yet what he expects from the future. "My mom and dad both have interesting jobs," he says. "My dad likes being a lawyer and my mom likes being an editor. I don't know what I'd like to be, though. That seems like so far away, it's hard to think about.

"I am sort of looking forward to high school—not next year, but the year after that. I don't know for sure which one I'll go to—it de-

While Patrick feels secure at home, he admits that he sometimes feels sad when people stare at him in public.

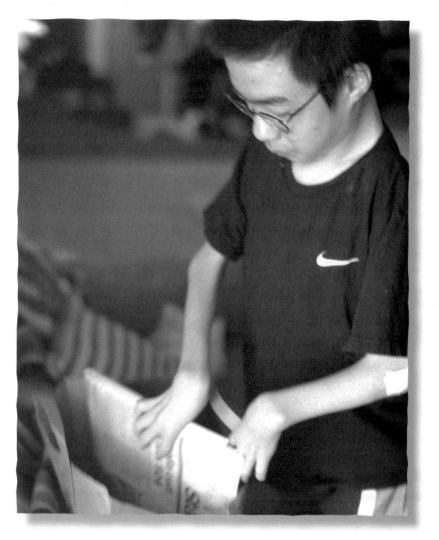

pends on the programs they have for disabled kids, I guess. Ben and Em go to different high schools, and they're happy where they are.

"When I'm grown up, I think I want to get married. I want to have kids of my own—I'd like to be a dad. Sometimes I do wonder about being older and needing help, though. I think about getting dressed, and not knowing how to tie shoes, and stuff like that. I might talk to Em about that—she has arthrogryposis, too. I bet she's thought about it."

WHAT'S POSSIBLE, WHAT ISN'T

Patrick says that his parents have told him not to assume that his limits today will be his limits of tomorrow.

"They remind me that there were things I couldn't do before because of my disability," he says. "And today I can. Like, I used to not be able to climb stairs in our house, and now I can."

His mother nods. "It's because of the leverage," she says. "There came a time when suddenly he could do stairs. His legs had gotten long enough where he didn't have to bend his right knee as much as before, and all of a sudden it worked. So who knows what he'll be able to accomplish later on?

"So we never say what he'll be able to do and what he won't. Certainly the vast majority of adults I've encountered with AMC live independently. Some have an aide that comes in the morning; many are married. Patrick hasn't personally met any adults with his disability, but I think he's getting to an age where that will become interesting to him, expand his horizons a bit. But most of all, it will show him that there are many choices he will have in life."

"A PEOPLE PERSON"

One thing which will serve him well in life, she says, is his generous, caring nature.

"It's his greatest asset," his mother maintains. "He's totally aware of other people's feelings. He's polite; he's thoughtful. I guess you could say Patrick's got all the social graces. He's got a talent for just sensing the mood, the situation, and knowing how to behave.

"He's grateful for help, if someone does something for him, or for the family in general—and he'll make a point of sincerely thanking them. He's wise beyond his years, I think."

Patrick shrugs. "I'm a people person," he says. "I really like watching people, thinking about what they are doing, why they act like they act. I like to talk to people, and especially I like to laugh. I know my family has told me I have good people skills—I don't know. I just try to be understanding and get along with everybody."

"I'D HAVE TO THINK ABOUT THAT"

He brightens, remembering something. "I just thought of something else I would wish for, besides winning a million dollars and buying sports cars. I'd wish that some company made cool shoes like Jordans, you know, but ones that would fit over my braces.

"See, I have to get wide shoes all the time, otherwise my leg braces don't fit. I'd want black ones, if I had a choice—that would look cool. But it seems like the only shoes that are really cool are too narrow."

But wouldn't it be easier just to wish that he didn't have AMC, not having to deal with all the difficulties and inconveniences?

"Maybe," he says, thinking hard. "I'm not sure. See, I'm used to being this way. I'm used to the kind of joints and stuff I have. This is me. So I don't know if I'd like being a different person. I don't know—I'd have to think about that."

"MY DISABILITY HAS MADE ME
STRONGER. EVERY DAY I FACE
NEW CHALLENGES."

It's difficult to imagine anyone not liking Angie, a fifteen-year-old with long ash-blonde hair. She's lively and talkative, with an engaging smile and a quick wit. Like other girls her age, she can be loud and giggly, and she seems used to having adults remind her to keep her voice down occasionally.

"I can't help it," she grins. "I like to talk! I know I should be quieter, but sometimes, I just think of something I want to say. And so I say it—much to my teachers' displeasure, I guess. My problem is I have too much fun with my friends!"

Having been born with cerebral palsy (CP), Angie walks with more difficulty than others her age, requiring leg braces for stability. She also has a lazy eye, which is disconcerting at first.

"I know," she says. "It seems like I'm looking over your shoulder, instead of your face, right? That's part of the CP, I guess. But I'm not complaining; there are a lot of people with CP that have worse things than I do."

TWO MONTHS EARLY

There are various causes of cerebral palsy, says Angie, and there's no way of knowing for sure what caused hers.

"It can be something that happens before birth or during birth," she says. "I guess it can even result from something when you're young, too, but mine isn't that. Anyway, cerebral palsy is a lack of muscle control; it can mean that you walk clumsy, or your balance isn't so good. Some people with CP can have trouble speaking, or they might be blind. Like I said, mine isn't as bad as a lot of people's.

"I was born two months early, and my lungs and my heart were what they call severely underdeveloped," she explains. "That means that they would only work with help from machines and stuff. I was due to be born on Halloween, but I arrived on August 19. What a surprise for everyone!

"The doctors didn't know right away that I had cerebral palsy, though. A big reason for CP is some trauma at birth, like not getting enough oxygen, I guess. Anyway, that's what probably happened to me, but they didn't diagnose me until later. When I was born, they were just concentrating on keeping me alive."

"THEY BAPTIZED ME REALLY QUICK"

The doctors in the intensive care unit could not offer many reassurances to her parents, Angie says.

Angie, who was born two months prematurely, was diagnosed with cerebral palsy when she was nine months old.

"They told my mom and dad that I'd probably die," she sighs. "The doctors said that if I did live, there was a good chance I'd be a vegetable or something. They figured I had a day or so to live, and I was on all kinds of heart monitors and oxygen and everything—just to keep me breathing and alive. My heart kept stopping, I guess; that was a big problem in the first few weeks I was alive.

"My parents baptized me really quick. They didn't have a name picked out yet—I mean, I wasn't supposed to even be here yet! So they baptized me 'Mary,' and later, when they'd had a little more time to think about it, changed it to Angela. My mom told me that she'd been praying so hard for me when I was in the hospital, and my grandma had been, too. So I guess they figured I was going to be an angel pretty quick; that's where the Angela came from."

She grins. "Most of my friends would laugh if they heard me called Angela. It's usually Angie. Of course, I answer to almost anything—even 'Hey, you!'"

DIAGNOSING ANGIE

Angie defied the odds, however. She was finally released from the hospital, although her parents were instructed to keep a close eye on her breathing. Besides that, she says, it was just a matter of waiting to see what effects the trauma of being a premature baby had caused.

"It was about nine months later that they knew I had CP. They could tell because of the way my feet turned way in—they just couldn't straighten out. I was cross-eyed, and didn't have very good eye-hand coordination. I couldn't move my left hand quick, like I can my right hand. In fact, my left-handed abilities pretty much sucked.

"They got me in AFOs pretty quick after that," she explains. "That's what we call these braces—AFO stands for ankle foot or-thoses. Anyway, I've been in them ever since. I have to wear mine pretty much all the time. I know some kids who don't wear them every day, but I need the stability.

"Actually, the doctors told my parents that my AFOs would eventually get smaller, that I wouldn't need these that go up so far. But I really doubt that's going to happen. I've seen people that have small ones, just more down by their ankles. But I think I'd have trouble walking unless they came up higher."

So Many Surgeries

Asked if doctors have done any operations to correct some of the effects of CP, Angie laughs.

"I have had so many surgeries; I can't even start! I had one to correct being cross-eyed—that kind of resulted in the lazy eye I told you about before. My parents had to do these exercises with me, hold their finger up, and I had to follow it with my eyes, without moving my head at all. Oh, that was so hard!" she exclaims. "I couldn't ever do it, not at all.

"Anyway, that was when I was three. The doctors tightened up the muscles of my eyes so they wouldn't turn in. My parents used to tell me a funny story about how I came out of the surgery. I guess the doctors gave me some strange eyedrops and stuff, stronger than even morphine. And when they wheeled me out after surgery, I looked so spaced out. My parents said, 'Oh my gosh—our daughter is high!'"

Angie had other surgeries to loosen muscles in her tight ankles. "My ankles were so tight I couldn't bend them at all," she says. "I had to have that one twice, because the doctors had goofed up the first time. Anyway, after my ankle cords were loosened, I had heel cords stretched out, to increase my mobility. I've had pins in my ankles—first put in, then later surgically removed. Plates in my hips."

She looks up at the ceiling, trying to keep them all straight. "They rearranged muscles in my knee. And later this summer, I'm having another operation. One of my legs is two inches longer than the other, so they're going to shorten it."

She shudders. "They're going to *break it* and then shorten it. Yuck."

A Family in Turmoil

In addition to growing up with physical challenges caused by her birth defect, Angie also had to deal with a family that was in serious crisis.

"It started a long time before I was born," she says. "My mom did drugs before she got pregnant with me. And after I was born. She didn't use them when she was pregnant, she's told me that. The drug she used was heroin, much different than marijuana and very addictive.

"My dad used drugs, too, but mostly he was a drinker. He even now is a drinker—he has to have a beer every morning or else his hands really shake."

While Angie has faced many physical challenges because of her disability, she has also endured numerous family problems.

This is difficult for Angie to talk about; she is fiercely loyal to her family, even though she knows that they have made mistakes. "I don't remember being really happy at home when I was little. I loved my mom and dad, though. She worked at night and my dad worked as a machinist during the day, so someone was always home with me. I remember that my mom was always so depressed, so sad when she was using. It seemed like there was nothing she really wanted to do, you know? I was little then, but I remember really well. It was like she was so tired, she couldn't get interested or excited about anything."

CHILD PROTECTION

When she was in preschool, Angie and her ten-year-old brother were taken away from their parents.

"It was Child Protective Services that did it," she explains. "And I don't exactly know how it all happened—see, I was only four. We were taken away because, well, partly because of drugs, and partly because Child Protection thought my parents were neglecting me. But, they weren't.

"See, I know about this because of my brother, what he's told me. Dustin was ten when it happened, so he remembers more details. I've heard different versions of this of course, and I guess who you're talking to makes a difference. I mean, Uncle Wally says one thing; my mom says something else; my brother, my dad—you know what I mean? So everyone is like saying their own version of what really happened. But here is what I think happened:

"I don't know how Child Protection got brought into it. Maybe my preschool. See, in my family, dark circles under the eyes is sort of a hereditary thing. See how my eyes are real dark under here? Well, when I was in preschool, some teacher or other must have told them it seemed like I must not be getting any sleep, because I looked like this. And plus, I was really, really skinny. I ate like a bird. So it must have looked like no one was taking care of me."

A CIGARETTE BURN

The idea that a child was being neglected was enough reason to get Child Protective Services involved, but Angie says another incident made things worse.

"A couple of days before they came out to the house to do their interview or evaluation or whatever they do, I had a cigarette burn on my forehead. I didn't walk back then—I couldn't walk until I was six, because of my cerebral palsy—I was still crawling. Anyway, I crawled into my dad's cigarette and burned myself.

"The Child Protection people asked if my daddy burned me, and I told them yes. I mean, he had burned me—but I didn't mean it the way they interpreted it. I didn't understand what they meant by the words 'on purpose,' so I agreed, I guess. And that was the reason I was taken, and my brother was, too.

"I remember the night before we were taken, my mom was crying really hard. I told her not to be sad, not to cry. I remember that really well. I didn't know they were going to take me out of my house, away from my parents. I was just trying to cheer her up because she was so sad, you know? But my mom knew. She knew it was going to happen; she just didn't know exactly when we'd be taken.

"Anyway, the Child Protection people came to take me away at school. I think Dustin was in fourth grade—and they took him out of school, too. I don't remember too much about it actually happening. That's funny, isn't it? You'd think I'd remember details like that, but I don't.

"I do remember that I got taken to a children's shelter called St. Joseph's for a time. I had a social worker then, I remember that. I

At the age of four, Angie was taken away from her parents by Child Protective Services, which accused her parents of neglect.

know I was so sad, because I missed Dustin. I kept wondering where he was, and worrying because I didn't know if I was going to get to see him again. I was so close to him, see?"

WITH UNCLE WALLY

Angie wasn't in the home very long before she was visited by her mother's brother and his wife.

"That would be Uncle Wally and Aunt Fran," she says. "They came to get me, to let me live with them, at least for a while. And yeah, I knew them from before; it wasn't like they were strangers or anything. They had babysat me sometimes, before all this happened. They took my brother, too, from wherever he'd been placed.

"So it was the four of us: Dustin and me, and Aunt Fran and Uncle Wally. But then a couple of years ago, they got divorced, and she moved out. So Uncle Wally's been the one I've been with. Even now, it's just the two of us, since Dustin is old enough to be out on his own. The two of us, and my cat and my dog."

Angie says that her parents have had their problems since then. "My dad was actually in prison," she says. "It was for selling drugs. In fact, some people in our family say that's how my mom got addicted, but I don't know. I can't say. But that was when I was in fourth grade, that he went to prison. I guess one good thing came of that—he had to stop drinking, for awhile, anyway."

WORKING THINGS OUT

Angie says that although her father was released after two years, he returned to prison soon afterwards.

"It wasn't for going back to selling drugs," she says. "He violated his parole. See, you have to promise certain things when you get out of jail—not to hang around with criminals after you get out, and you have to promise to check in with your parole officer. Anyway, he didn't check in with his halfway house regularly like he was supposed to. So back in."

Angie looks sad. "I love my dad a lot. But he missed a lot of my life, four years. That's a huge amount in a kid's life. I see him now; he's out of jail. He's still a machinist, and he doesn't do drugs anymore. But he still drinks a lot.

"My mom worked hard to get off her drug habit. She's been through the methadone program, and she's off antidepressants. She's done really well about getting straight, I think."

"I GUESS I'D CHOOSE UNCLE WALLY"

Angie insists that even though it is not a common thing for a teen to live with an uncle rather than both parents, she is happy with the arrangement.

"I see my parents on the weekends, usually. I'm buddies with my dad; we get along fine. I'm friends with my mom; she and I talk on the phone every day. She's been clean for a couple years now, and that's great. It's a little harder to stay in touch with my dad, though, because he doesn't have a phone or a car. I can't just decide to call him up on the spur of the moment or have him come over to see me. So that part's hard.

"Wally is a good guy," she says. "I mean, he's like a father, basically. I'm at the age when I could have some input with a judge into where I live, who'd have custody of me, I guess. But even though I'm really close to both my parents now, I'm happy where I am.

"In a way," she confides, "I'm kind of scared to leave. I'd miss Uncle Wally, because I've been living with him for eleven years now. I'm used to him."

What's he like?

Angie shrugs.

"He's real quiet most of the time," she says. "Like if I'm sitting out in front of the house talking to a friend, he'll walk by without saying anything. But if you say hi, he'll say hi back. He's a good guy; he doesn't try to boss me around usually. We have fights sometimes, but it's just like any family, I guess. We disagree over me being on the phone all the time, stuff like that. I'm just used to him."

"I LIKE BEING FIFTEEN MOST OF THE TIME"

As for her life in general, Angie says she's pretty happy. "I like being fifteen most of the time," she smiles. "I have a lot of friends at school; some of them I've known since junior high and elementary school. I'm used to them, and they're used to me; that's important, I think. And I have a variety of friends, a big old variety!

"I love talking on the phone (just ask Uncle Wally!) and just hanging out. If I go over to a friend's house after school, I usually just ride the bus home with them. Uncle Wally doesn't like to drive a whole lot, but if I get in a bind, he will. I have some friends who have cars, so that's even better!

Angie, who has lived with her uncle for eleven years, says she's happy with the arrangement, though occasionally, she admits, "we disagree over me being on the phone all the time."

"I'm going to turn sixteen next summer, but I'm truthfully not in any big hurry to drive. I mean, some kids can hardly wait—it means more independence and everything. I totally understand that, but for me, I think it's kind of scary. Maybe I'll feel different when I'm actually sixteen, but for now I'm not even sure I'll learn to drive. I mean, as long as I have friends that do, I can have a lot of fun just going around with them."

ADAPTED SPORTS

Angie says that her friends have been the most important part of her life over the past few years.

"Some of them aren't disabled, but I have a lot who are. Some of my best disabled friends are kids I know from the sports teams I play on, the adapted sports. A lot of people are kind of shocked when disabled kids talk about being on sports teams, but that's really common at my high school. We have a blast! The teams from my school are called the Tigers, and I've got pictures of my teams all over my room.

"There's leagues for mentally disabled kids, too, but not at my particular school—I think those kids play at Roosevelt. But physically

Angie plays on a hockey team for physically disabled teens and says she has met some of her best friends through adapted sports.

disabled kids have the POHI division—that's Physical or Other Handicap Impairments. We've got a lot of variety in our disabilities, too. I mean, there's kids that have CP like me, muscular dystrophy, brain injuries, seizures, and some who are deaf. For those kids there's a person who can do signing to help those kids.

"There are a bunch of different sports teams, depending on the season. I play soccer, floor hockey, and softball, and they're all fun, believe me. The rule is you have to have at least two people in wheelchairs on the field (or the floor, depending on the game) at any given time. Like in soccer, we use wheelchairs back by the crease, defensively. It makes it hard for the other team to score a goal if we've got people in wheelchairs going back and forth across the goal, you know? They really block the shots."

"SCHOOL IS SOMETIMES REALLY HARD FOR ME"

Angie is not quite as exuberant when describing her academic classes in high school, although she says she gets decent grades.

"I take mostly mainstream classes—that means with all kids, not just disabled," she says. "For me, though, the CP has made a few problems. I mean, I have some brain damage, although nowhere near what the doctors had first thought!

"In fact," she laughs, "they were all saying I'd never be able to talk. And my mom and dad and my uncle all say I never shut up! I talk, I laugh, I sing, I do it all. But I have some learning problems.

"It's not remembering; I have a really good memory. But I get distracted very easily, and I tend to get all stressed and worried if I have more than one task ahead of me. Like if I have a test coming up in one class, and an essay or something to write for another. I just freeze; I can't do anything. It happens all the time.

"I just get overloaded, even though really it isn't all that much work. That's my biggest problem, and for a high school kid, it can really get in the way. I mean, it's pretty common to have assignments in more than one class, right?"

MAKING ADJUSTMENTS

"I also learn a little slower; I know that's true. And combined with the distraction thing, teachers are generally pretty good about giving me a little more time for things than other kids. I think they're more interested in what I'm learning than how fast I can get it on the paper, you know?

"The support class for disabled kids at the end of the day helps, too. The teacher helps you get structured, and gives you help getting started; sometimes that's all the help I need. Really, the only class where I'm not mainstreamed is phys ed."

Angie sighs. "Although, sometimes I wish I could get out of certain classes. Like biology—I'm so bummed that we have to dissect a fetal pig next week! I get nightmares just thinking about that.

Conquering her fears, Angie dissects a pig during biology class, one of the mainstream classes that Angie attends.

"My best subject, though, is English," she says, beaming. "I'm going to take a lot of poetry next year, two trimesters of it. Also a creative writing class. That's fun for me. I mean, not so much the writing of poetry (although I'd really like to get better at that) but reading it. I absolutely love Shel Silverstein's poems. I just like the whole idea of having a special way of looking at things, which is what poetry basically is.

"I did get a big compliment from another teacher earlier this year," she says proudly. "We had to do a timeline of our lives in world studies. We handed them in, and when the teacher gave it back later, she had written, 'Angela, you have been through so much in such a short time—you are truly amazing.'"

She grins. "That was so cool! I cried, I was so proud, you know? It just made feel so good."

"It's All About Them"

Asked if she ever has felt ostracized because of her disability, she looks puzzled.

"Of course, yeah," she says. "I mean, I think everyone with a disability has gotten mocked or laughed at or ignored at some point. But the thing is, when people are cruel, you have to remember that it has nothing at all to do with you. I mean, it doesn't.

"See, when people are mean to me, it's all about them. Their need for self-gratification. Like it makes them feel big and important or whatever. They don't feel very good about themselves, or they wouldn't do it. Tearing me down, or whatever, is the only way they can feel important."

"Most of the Kids . . . Are Great"

"Most of the kids at my high school are great; they're friendly even if they don't personally know you. Like this one time, I was walking to the elevator to go upstairs; I go kind of slow, you know. And I dropped something out of my lunch. I think it was my cheese.

"Anyway, this one guy came up and picked it up for me. I thanked him and got into the elevator. And he walked up the stairs. And then when I got upstairs, I dropped my apple!"

Angie giggles, remembering. "And there that same boy was again, picking it up for me. I'm sure he thought I was like doing it on purpose, flirting with him or something. Like those ladies who used to drop their handkerchiefs on purpose so a guy would bring it to them. I felt like such a jerk!"

Thelma and Louise

Angie acknowledges that the comments and mocking has made more introverted disabled teens stay away from public places.

"Not me, though," she says. "I go to the mall, wherever. I'll even split up with a friend if she wants to go to one store and I want to go to another. I don't care. I'm used to it.

"Sure, it gets to me sometimes—I'd be lying if I said it didn't. Like if someone says something, or you can hear kids talking about you. But I try to remember what I told you: it isn't about me. It's them.

"Now, the girl who's going to be my stepsister—when my dad gets remarried, which he's going to soon—she'll take people on who do that to me. Her name is Jessica. My dad calls us Thelma and Louise when we're together, because we can be really assertive. When I'm with her, I'm really a lot braver than I feel when I'm on my own."

Limited Choices in Shoes

Besides enduring insensitive people, Angie says she gets irritated at the scarcity of styles when it comes to buying shoes.

"I know other disabled kids feel this way, too," she says. "I don't want to wear old-lady shoes. But boy, there's nothing there for teenagers! I love going shopping, but I hate going to shoe stores.

"I think that's one reason why I wear pants more than dresses—there are such dorky shoes. They have to be wide to fit in my braces, see? And these wintery shoes are okay with pants," she says, lifting her pant leg to reveal dark brown, rubber-soled shoes. "But can you imagine these with a skirt?

"My feet aren't really very big, but my shoes look huge. It's just because the braces take up so much space. The shoes have to be so wide, it's not even funny.

"I'm probably going to be asked to prom this year—the boy I've been going out with is a senior—but what will I do? I can borrow a friend's dress; maybe it will be long enough so they can't see my shoes. I don't know. It's little stuff like that; I mean, it seems little. But those are the things that are so frustrating to me."

Angie says she will most likely go to the prom this year, but she worries about the limited choices in shoes she'll have to wear with her dress.

"I'M REALLY HARD ON MY BRACES"

Could she ever take her braces off and walk, or are they absolutely necessary?

"I do take them off sometimes at home," she says. "It really feels good sometimes. But really, I can't walk much without them. One time I broke one at school—I mean it just broke. You could hear the thing go *crack*, so loud! So I took it off for the rest of the day.

"My ankles are so weak, though, it took me forever to get around. I mean, I walk really slowly, even with the braces. But without them, it was absolutely no good. I tend to be really hard on my braces—the guy who fits them says he's never seen anyone go through them like I do. I've broken several. I guess it's just wear and tear. It's not like I'm trying to break them or anything."

IMAGINING THE FUTURE

Angie says she is having fun being a teenager, but she sometimes thinks ahead to graduating from high school.

"You can't help but think ahead," she says. "I mean, already we take tests to show our aptitude for different things, to give us an idea of careers. We took one thing called a PLAN test—it kind of measures your interest in different areas.

"My strong points on the PLAN test were working with people in some health-related field. I guess that's accurate, too, because I sometimes think about being a physical therapist, or a counselor or something. I love little kids and babies; maybe something to do with them would be really challenging and fun.

"But I also love poetry, so maybe I'd do that on the side or something. I'm pretty sure no one makes a living writing poems, but it would be a good thing to have as a hobby or something.

"I see myself maybe getting married someday, too," she says. "It wouldn't be for a long time, though. The boy I go out with, Mark, is two years older than me. He's got CP, too. I have no idea how serious I am about him, but who knows? For right now, we have fun together."

"I HATE THE SMELL OF HOSPITALS"

The near future will bring another operation, and Angie has mixed feelings about it.

"Really," she says, "I hate the smell of hospitals. You'd think I'd be used to it by now, having been in them so often. But I'm not. The minute I walk in and I smell that cleaner, or whatever it is they use, I gag.

"But on the other hand, the operation will help with my foot and knee turning in. I was getting better, doing things easier until that happened. I don't mean my CP was going away, because you don't ever get over it. But I was getting used to moving in a certain way, and it was easier for me than it had been in a long time.

"But then this stiffness happened. And I know when things like this have happened before, the operation really does make a difference, makes moving easier. So even though it means smelling that gross hospital smell, it'll be worth it."

"I CARE ABOUT OTHER PEOPLE"

Angie says that she recently had to assess her strengths and weaknesses for one of her classes. To her friends, she laughs, none of what she learned was much of a surprise.

"It's kind of like my strengths and weaknesses are the same," she says. "As far as strengths go, I like people—I love people. I'm interested in them, and I care about them. And that brings me to my weakness; I talk too much, I get too involved or something. I'd rather talk than do homework, or listen to the teacher, or whatever!

"I know there is a downside to that, because I realize I can't always help people. Like there was this one girl—she's disabled. Her mother died when the girl was seven, and she just can't handle it, you know? She like follows me around, talking to me all the time. I tried to listen, but she was so needy—and I didn't have any answers for her. She's at Courage Center now because she tried to kill herself. I feel bad about that—some things are just too much for friends, I guess. Maybe they'll help her sort out her problems there."

ADVICE TO ANY TEENS WITH DISABILITIES

Angie says that if a teenager with a disability asked for advice, she'd simply say to hang in there. "That sounds dumb, but it's true," she maintains. "I think things get better as you go along—even for kids who don't cope with a disability very well at first.

"I was a speaker not too long ago at a class that some teachers were taking. I told them that my disability has made me stronger. Every day I face new challenges, and I try not to chicken out just because they're new, you know what I mean?

"Like for instance, I went rock climbing," she announces. "Me! It was so awesome. The whole thing was my hockey coach's idea. It was at a place that had a lot of activities like that, and I got to wear a safety belt, so I wouldn't get hurt. But still, you felt like every little step was huge.

Angie faces new challenges every day. "I try not to chicken out just because they're new."

"I hadn't intended to do it; I was just watching everyone try it, and the coach says, 'Angie, why don't you do it?' And I thought, 'Why not?' My legs kept slipping, but I have pretty strong arms from being in a wheelchair when I was younger, before I had leg braces. So that helped. But I was so proud of myself!"

Angie grins. "That's what I'd tell anyone, and I guess it doesn't matter whether the person has a disability or not. Just keep trying!"

Cindy

"I'M GRATEFUL I HAVE A FAMILY THAT CARES FOR ME ENOUGH TO HELP ME THE WAY THEY DO!"

I'm supposed to meet Cindy for the first time at 9:45 in one of her classrooms, but she's not there. The high school is bustling with activity as teenagers head to classes or lockers. Barb, a teacher who works exclusively with students with special needs, checks her watch and shakes her head.

"Cindy?" she says, with a hint of a smile. "Knowing her, she's probably down the hall, talking with her friends, and has lost all track of time."

She strides down a side hallway, and there, enclosed in a circle of laughing, talking teenagers, is a strikingly pretty girl in a wheelchair. Barb comes up behind her and lays a hand on her shoulder.

"Cindy," she says sternly, "when you make appointments, it's important to show up on time, okay?"

Flashing Barb an apologetic smile, Cindy turns the red and black chair deftly and extends her hand.

"Sorry about that," she says with an apologetic giggle. "I'm Cindy. Come on back to the classroom; we can talk in there."

SPINAL MUSCULAR ATROPHY

Cindy heads back to the classroom and finds a comfortable corner. She places the notebook and little silver tape recorder she'd been carrying on a nearby bookcase.

"I've got a form of muscular dystrophy," she explains. "The type I have is known as SMA—infant spinal muscular atrophy. Basically, it's a condition that affects my muscles, making them weaker. I was born with it.

68

"It brings breathing problems after a while, because it takes muscles to breathe, you know, to make your lungs work. I have to have breathing treatments every day, because of that. I only use about 75 percent of my lung capacity, I think. And so sometimes, after I've been talking for awhile, I kind of run out of breath."

Because she was born with SMA, does that mean that doctors knew right away that she had it?

Cindy shakes her head. "No, I had some problems right off, but they didn't find out about the SMA until I was about eighteen months old. I was born with a clubfoot—do you know what that is? It's like when your foot is turned way in, at a real sharp angle. And that was just the beginning."

Cindy was born with a form of muscular dystrophy, a condition that weakens her muscles and affects her breathing.

"My Parents Knew Something Was Wrong"

Cindy says her parents knew there was something wrong with their new baby, besides just having a clubfoot.

"I'm the youngest of three kids," she says. "And my mom and dad felt like they understood something about babies! I mean, like how they develop, what's normal, and what seems different. And it seemed like I was going at a lot slower pace than my brother or sister had.

"I was really fussy, always spitting up. Now, we know that was because the muscles at the top of my stomach had deteriorated, and it was hard to take food. I mean, she'd feed me like an ounce of formula, and it would come right back out! That scared my mom, I know.

"And I wasn't developing right, either," she continues. "I was slow to sit up, and when I did, I was real floppy. But when my mom would mention these things to the pediatrician, he'd just say I was going at my own rate. They told her she was being overprotective, and that I was fine."

Devastating News

But while doctors seemed unconcerned about Cindy's eating difficulties and slow development, her mother was persistent.

"She just knew something wasn't right," says Cindy. "And she finally took me to a different pediatrician, who believed her, took her seriously, I guess. Anyway, this pediatrician had me see a specialist, who ended up taking a biopsy of one of my leg muscles.

"That was the only way they could really tell what was going on," she says. "And when they looked at that muscle under the microscope or whatever, they could diagnose what was wrong with me. And that's when they figured out it was SMA."

Cindy says that the doctors then explained to her parents that her condition was genetic. "It takes a gene from both parents," she says. "Someone on both my father's side and someone on my mother's had this, like a hundred years ago, I guess. I think my parents felt fortunate that my brother and sister weren't born with it, too.

"My mom has told me about that time, when they first found out. I know she and my dad were really devastated, really afraid for me. I guess when you have a new baby, you just don't think you'll have to deal with this stuff. It took them by surprise."

"I Have Type II"

Cindy says that there are three levels of SMA—the first being the most severe. "In type I, that's the worst. Kids die very early, like by two years old. See, the atrophy of their muscles affects everything from swallowing to breathing, and they can't manage things like that as the disease makes the muscles weaker.

"I have type II, which isn't as bad—but bad enough! My type usually means that a child lives to about age ten or so. But I'm almost twenty—so I'm beating the odds, I guess! But learning that their baby was going to probably die by the time she was ten really shattered my mom and dad.

"Type III is mildest of the three. From what I understand, people who have this type don't have their breathing muscles affected as much. Although, I think all three types—even type III—require you to be in a wheelchair. I think everyone with SMA is, at least everyone I've ever seen."

Cindy says that the wheelchair often gives people the wrong impression about her disability, however. "I can't walk, it's true," she says. "But I'm not paralyzed. I can feel my legs; lots of people assume that it's like a spinal injury, and it's not. I can move my legs, but I can't pick them up to walk. It's a muscular thing; I can't use my muscles to support my body or to hold myself up.

"My arms are okay for now. I can lift my right arm higher than the left. I know some people with SMA who don't have much use of their arms. I think to me, the biggest mistake people can make with SMA is to assume what they can't or can do. I think it all depends on the person; everyone's unique. I mean, look at me—if you look at the statistics for type II SMA, I've almost doubled my life expectancy!"

"I Remember Walking"

Cindy's disability was not as severe when she was younger. In fact, she says, she remembers walking when she was little.

"I know I walked for awhile," she says. "I learned later than most kids, but I did walk. It was fun, being able to do more things. But it was tiring, because it was so hard for me. And then, when walking got too hard, I used a walker for awhile, for stability. And then I just stopped being able to walk.

"I had both hips operated on when I was about seven. That's the point where I wasn't able to walk anymore. See, the tissue in my hips was deteriorating, and the doctors put pins in to hold the bones in place. I think they did one, and waited a few weeks and did the other one.

"Anyway, after my hip operations, I never walked again—that's what my dad told me. I'd been able to walk a little before then, but afterwards, it was impossible."

Cindy smiles. "You know something funny? In my dreams, I'm always walking. Or running, or skating, or stuff like that. I don't even ever remember my chair showing up in any of my dreams! Isn't that weird?"

LIMITS

Being confined to a wheelchair has other effects besides an inability to walk, Cindy says. Because of her limited lung capacity, she needs breathing treatments every day, both at home and at school.

"I use two machines," she says. "We've got both of them at home, so I don't need to go to the doctor or a hospital or anything. This is just basic daily operation for me. The first thing is a nebulizer, a mask I wear to inhale moist air. People with asthma use nebulizers for the same reason, because it helps open your lungs so they work more efficiently. Nebulizer treatments take awhile each day, about ten or fifteen minutes each. I have nebulizer treatments at home and at school.

"There's another machine I use, too, called an IPPB [Intermittent Positive Pressure Breathing]. It's like a pressure thing, I guess is the best way to describe it. Whereas the nebulizer is a mask, the IPPB is like a straw I put in my mouth. When you breathe in, it forces your lungs to open. That machine I don't bring to school, just because it's so darn heavy. It isn't really that big, just bulky. Plus, the IPPB treatments take longer—about half an hour, usually.

"I'm at a big risk for pneumonia," she says matter-of-factly. "I guess I'd have to say that I could die from a case of that, just because my lungs aren't as efficient as they should be. So when people are sick, they don't come around. Even in my family, if someone is sick, they usually don't come into contact with me unless they wear a mask or something. So I've got to be careful, because even a little thing like a cold could become dangerous for me."

"I USED TO GET SO FRUSTRATED"

Cindy says that when she was younger, the confinement of the wheelchair was often very frustrating.

Cindy's sister Becky assists her with a nebulizer, a device that helps open Cindy's lungs to make breathing easier. "This is just basic daily operation for me," says Cindy, who receives nebulizer treatments at home and at school.

"I don't think it was so bad at home with my family," she says, remembering. "I have pretty happy memories about growing up with my brother and sister, and about being in our house. And yeah, maybe there were a lot of things I couldn't do, but there were more things that I *could* do, I think.

"I went to preschool and kindergarten. Those were special ed classes, and not just for kids in wheelchairs. In fact, I'm pretty sure I was the only kid with SMA; in fact, I'm sure I was. There was a variety of kids with different sorts of problems, and that was okay. But I was mainstreamed starting in first grade, and I made a lot of friends.

"The one thing that got me mad—actually, the first real time I can remember being angry about being in the chair—was when I couldn't go to a friend's house. Maybe there were too many stairs or maybe going inside some houses would be a problem. Back then, I had a manual chair, and my parents (or theirs) could carry me inside, and then get the wheelchair set up. But some friends had houses that were too small or something. I don't know, that was always so disappointing."

She seems lost in thought for a moment, then smiles. "Oh, well, I guess I just invited them over to my house. I suppose that's how I dealt with it."

Getting "Pushed"

Though Cindy is a very outgoing young woman today, she acknowledges that she was not always so. In fact, she says, she was too shy and quiet as a youngster.

"A lot of who I am is because of my parents," she says truthfully. "They refused to spoil me or treat me like I was helpless. I think because they were both afraid for me when I was diagnosed with type II SMA, they wanted me to do as much as I could, for as long as I could—you know? 'Live life to the fullest,' my mom would say.

"They expected me to try things, to work hard. Sometimes I'd get really mad at how little they'd help me do things, but now I see it was because they wanted me to push myself. Like if I'd drop something, my mom would say, 'Cindy, you pick that glass up.' I'd say, 'Mom, I can't!' But she wouldn't buy that; she still doesn't. She makes me accountable for myself. Just because I'm in a chair doesn't mean I don't have responsibilities."

Overcoming Shyness

Cindy gives credit to her special education classes for helping her become more outgoing, something that many disabled kids have trouble being, she says.

"A lot of disabled kids try to just stay out of the way," she says. "They don't say a word; they don't want to call any more attention to themselves than they already are by having a chair, or braces, or whatever. It's like they don't want to be noticed.

"I was like that when I was younger, too. But the educational assistants—we call them EAs—try to get you out of that way of

Crediting her family and special education classes, Cindy says she has learned to become more outgoing and confident.

thinking. They want you to be as independent as you can and to do as much as you can until you're tired.

"The support class I'm in now helps you learn to speak up. There's a lot of talking and helping one another, and that's good for everybody. Otherwise, you just have to accept what's going on around you, and sometimes it's not what you really want!

"My mom has always told me, 'I'm not going to be around forever, you know.' I don't like hearing her say that, but I appreciate what she's telling me. She's saying, 'Don't be content to just sit in your chair.'

"I think that message started finally getting through when I was in fifth or sixth grade. I'm not exactly sure," she says. "It didn't happen all at once or anything, but it just kind of turned out that more kids were being friendly, and I was talking more. And that really made school more fun!"

Cindy's mother has always encouraged her to be independent, telling her, "Don't be content to just sit in your chair."

"SOMETIMES PEOPLE CAN BE MEAN"

Generally, she says, she looks on the positive side of things but admits that there are times when her disability seems overwhelming. And when kids her own age are hurtful, it can feel devastating.

"I think younger kids are meaner than kids my age," she says. "If I think about the times I've had my feelings badly hurt, it was when I was younger. Like I remember at our old house, I had friends in the neighborhood that I really looked forward to seeing. But sometimes, when I'd go out looking for them, they'd see me coming in my chair and they'd run away, run into a house where they knew I couldn't follow them.

"My sister Becky has always stuck up for me when stuff like that happened and she saw it. If she'd been there when those kids did that, she'd have given them more than a piece of her mind.

And what made it hurt was that I thought they were my friends, and I just couldn't understand why they'd do that, you know?"

"Some People Only See the Chair"

"Some of the neighbor kids, the younger ones, are mean now," she says. "I have this one friend named Sonia; she has no arms. And her legs kind of end where our knees would be. She's like that because her mom and dad used drugs and alcohol while her mom was pregnant. Anyway, Sonia's really smart and funny, really nice. But sometimes when she comes over and we're sitting outside on the porch, the neighbor kids are like, 'Hey, who cut off your arms?'"

Adults are seldom mean, but they can be unintentionally cruel, she maintains. "I know my mom gets really mad when we go out sometimes and people stare. It is rude, but I'm more used to it, I think. What gets me mad is when we go to a restaurant and the waitress will ask my mom what *I* want! It's like people only see the chair, and they don't understand the person in it. Because I'm in a wheelchair, they think I'm retarded or deaf or something.

"Lots of times when a waitress says to my mom, 'And what will she have?' my mom will say, 'Ask her.' I'm glad she does this, but in a way it takes some of the fun of going out. And my parents can't fight my battles—I've got to do it. But sometimes it gets tiring having to fight the same ones all the time."

School

Cindy is a fifth-year senior in high school. Technically, she graduated last year, but returned for some classes she wasn't ready to take back then.

"The class I didn't take last year is called 'Transition Plus,'" she explains. "It's taught off campus; they teach you about job skills, what you need to know for interviewing, things like that. It's for kids with different disabilities.

"I had trouble thinking about off-campus classes last year; it was so hard to leave for the first three hours of the day and try to come back and jump back into my high school schedule, knowing what period it was and everything. I'd get confused where I was supposed to be; it just didn't work out for me. So I didn't do Transition Plus last year; instead I came back first semester and took it this year.

"This semester, I'm taking another off-campus class at the technical college downtown. It's not a disabled class; it's sort of an introduction to college. You learn about scheduling yourself, just getting used to what's going to happen when you're in college for real. And then, after that class, I come back to school here to finish up the day."

DAILY ROUTINES

In addition to having help from an EA at school, Cindy relies on help from a number of other people—most importantly, her family.

"People with SMA have what are called PCAs," she says. "That means personal care assistants. They're the people who help you with everything from medicines, treatments, dressing—you name it, they help with it.

"I'm lucky enough to have my brother Ian and my sister Becky be my PCAs. They're great! Ian is 25, and Becky is 21. And my mom and dad do a lot, too. Like my mom has to get up during the night and turn me, so I don't get muscle spasms from being in one position. She isn't really supposed to lift me, because she had back surgery not too long ago, but she knows just how to push so she doesn't hurt herself, I guess.

"My dad is the one who usually gets me up and dressed each morning; he's a mechanic and needs to get up really early anyway. And it takes me quite a while to get all my stuff done each day. So he's the lifter, basically. I'm usually up just after five each morning."

Is it difficult to depend on others for getting dressed and bathed?

Cindy shakes her head. "No, not at all," she says. "I mean, I'm used to it. That's the way my life is, so I can't think about it as something unusual or different. Privacy is not something I worry about. It's just everyday living for me. I'm grateful I have a family that cares for me enough to help me the way they do!"

"I'VE HAD A LOT OF CHAIRS"

The chair in which she spends her days is something of a marvel, Cindy says. "This is my fourth or fifth one, and yeah, it's pretty fancy. Like I said before, I started off with a manual one, you know, just one that someone either pushes you in or you move the wheels yourself. But the rest after that one have been electric, like this one.

"It's amazing how much some of these things cost!" she marvels. "I mean, this one was twenty-three thousand dollars. Luckily, insurance covers the costs most of the time; I don't know how anyone could afford something like this without insurance. I think the reason it's so much money is that it can tilt, which is what normal electric wheelchairs don't do. It's got a lot of features."

Why has she had so many chairs?

Cindy grins. "I don't really know," she says. "I don't think I'm hard on them or anything. But it's like, if it gets to where you need to repair it, and the repairs are going to add up to be almost more than a new one, it's time to get the new one. We've had a couple that have just broke. The last one I had was broken when I got it; the dealer called it a lemon when I brought it back and they looked at it.

"But the thing is," she says philosophically, "it's crucial that I have one that gets me around. I can't take it for granted. I live in the thing, you know? It's not like going out and getting a piece of furniture that's just for show. It's more than just a chair!"

Since most of her time is spent in her chair, Cindy stresses the importance of having a chair with the features that provide maximum mobility.

"I'D LIKE TO DRIVE"

Cindy says one of her dreams is to be able to drive a car, quite a step up from relying only on a wheelchair to get her places.

"I get rides when I need to go places; it isn't like I'm stuck all the time," she says. "I have a special school bus that picks me up, one with a lift for my chair. And our family van is customized for a wheelchair, too.

"But I'd really like to be able to drive myself. I don't get a lot of chances to be independent, so it would be great if I could. I'm in driver's education now, here at school. We're just using the simulators, you know? No behind-the-wheel stuff—that would come later. But for disabled people, it's a lot more complicated—you have to have a car that's been customized for your disability."

Cindy says that as a disabled student, she was urged to go to Courage Center to get an assessment of her potential to be a good driver, but she was dissatisfied with the results.

"I went to Courage Center a while back because my caseworker thought it would be a good idea. They have people there that know all about disabilities and what's available for cars, and they go over your particular case to see if you'd be able to drive safely. They test your reflexes, your eyesight, motor skills, stuff like that.

"But I wasn't happy with my time there, not at all. The guy I met with sort of stereotyped people with muscular dystrophy; he said that all kids with MD are unable to drive. He really wasn't very positive, and I went away from there thinking that was something I'd never do. I was really disappointed."

A GLIMMER OF HOPE

However, Cindy says, just recently she heard of a place that is more innovative in dealing with disabled drivers.

"I have a friend who had an assessment and was told, same as me, that he'd never be able to drive. They said his reflexes aren't quick enough, or strong enough, or something like that.

"Anyway, he found out that there's a place that just opened up that has more options. They have different steering wheels, smaller ones, that would be easier for someone with limited arm movement to use.

"When I heard about this, I wish the guy who did my assessment had been more open-minded and had tried some of these new steering wheels for me! I hate when people just make these blanket statements like, 'People with MD can't do this or that.' If everyone just obeyed stereoypes, nobody would try harder to push themselves, I think. Like I said, everyone is different, each case of MD is different."

DO DISABLED KIDS GET IN TROUBLE?

Teenagers are at a stage when it is common to rebel against parents, to test boundaries. How does that work for a young woman in a wheelchair?

Cindy laughs. "I get mad at people, just like any other kid," she says. "I fight with my parents, sure. And they get mad at me, too. I mean, don't think that my mom and dad treat me like some little princess or something; they'd laugh if anyone thought that. They expect things of me, just like they did when my brother and sister were my age.

Using her hand to support her arm, Cindy enjoys a cup of coffee at the neighborhood coffee shop.

"I don't have the ability to do the same things as another girl might when I get mad. I can't slam doors because in my house they're too heavy. Plus, it's hard to do that in a wheelchair! If I get really mad, I usually just go outside. We have a ramp, and that makes it easy to just go out the door, maybe around the block, or down to the coffee shop down the street. Just to blow off steam, you know?

"I think yelling at my parents is the worst I do. I don't swear at them or anything—and that doesn't have anything to do with whether or not I'm disabled. I just wouldn't do that; I wouldn't go over that line. The main thing is, I don't get any special treatment from anybody—not my family, not my teachers."

She smiles ruefully. "I get in trouble for not doing my homework, just like anybody else!"

PERSONAL CHALLENGES

However, there are aspects of her life that remind Cindy on a daily basis that she is *not* the same as everybody else—at least physically.

"I take a lot of medications," she acknowledges. "At least twelve in the morning and more in the evening when I get home. Some of it is preventative, you know, making sure I don't have lung problems. I guess that the pills are for a lot of different things.

"I'm on medication for seizures, I have these little ones, petit mal, I think they're called. Like a person with epilepsy might have. My mom says it's like I look like I'm asleep, and they only last a little while. But it's not something that I want to go through; in fact, if I wanted to drive, I'd have to make sure that they were under control.

"I had something more serious recently—cancer. I woke up one morning and was getting up for school, getting ready, you know? And I had this really horrible pain down deep in my abdomen. My parents took me into the hospital, and they found that I had cancer in one of my ovaries. I had it removed, and they say they got it all.

"It would be sad in someone who didn't have SMA, because it would mean that the person couldn't have children later on. But I'm not supposed to have kids—my lungs wouldn't let me survive childbirth, they say. So it's not a real loss for me—but scary. I'm not sure if having SMA increased the risk of getting cancer. I don't know if the doctors even know that; there's so much about my disability that they don't know enough about yet."

HAPPY THINGS

Cindy sighs as though the conversation has gotten too depressing. "Anyway, there are a lot of good things in my life," she says. "I don't know if people reading about me would think I should be sad, but I'm usually not. I've got lots of things that I'm happy about.

"I love going places, especially with my brother and sister. My dad or my brother just lifts me into the car, and we take off. My sister is especially fun to be around. We go to the mall, just out for walks, or whatever. I don't know what I'd do if I didn't have Becky to talk to. She's going to college now, to learn to be a nurse. I know she'll be a great one.

"One thing that was really fun—for my last birthday she took me out to one of the clubs. We had a ball," Cindy says, remembering. "I dance, yeah. Does that surprise you? Well, I try, anyway."

She laughs. "I don't move my chair or anything," she says. "I just, I don't know, I just move to the music. Maybe it looks kind of funny to someone watching me, but I don't care. I like to do it. It's the only way I can dance, so it's what I do. I usually don't get asked to dance, or anything. But it's fun being out on the floor with the music up loud."

LOTS OF GOOD THINGS

Cindy has a boyfriend, too, and that makes her happy.

"His name is Steve," she says, smiling. "He's got CP, cerebral palsy. He's in a wheelchair, too. He can walk but only for short distances, so he uses the chair. I met him playing adapted sports at my high school last year. Steve was on the other team, and we got to know each other.

"I went to prom with him last year; it was fun. He had a tux, and I had a new dress. I also went to an ROTC dance with him, a military ball, at his high school. He's a lot of fun to be around; all of my friends who know him think he's got a great sense of humor. My mom basically likes him; she just says he's loud sometimes. I guess he is, but I don't mind!"

Cindy says they enjoy a lot of the same things. "We like going to movies, which we do a lot," she says. "And we go have coffee, or just hang out and listen to music or whatever. It's nice that we don't have to have big plans to enjoy ourselves."

"It's Not Something I Can Plan On"

Cindy is unsure of what she will do when she finishes high school. She wants to go to college, she says, but she is undecided about what the future will hold.

"I used to want to be a nurse," she admits. "I think I was spending so much time in hospitals that it seemed like second nature or something! I thought, I could do this. I'd like to do something to help people.

"But realistically, I don't think it would work," she says. Although there is no known cure for SMA, Cindy says that there is a great deal of research going on. And while she doesn't dwell on it, the idea of life without SMA is intriguing.

"It's not something I can plan on," she says. "I know that. But there are things researchers are doing now to try to find out about SMA. I'm even participating in a study they're doing, a drug study. It's not to cure SMA, but they're trying to find ways to stop it or to at least slow its progress.

"In the study, some of the kids are given real pills, and the other group gets placebos—those are fake pills. You don't know which you have, and after the study is done, they measure the results, and see if the real ones worked. Everyone hopes, but no one knows what will happen."

Cindy says she and her boyfriend, Steve, share many of the same interests, such as going to the movies or having coffee together.

DIETING

One thing she knows, Cindy says, and that is that she must lose weight. She doesn't look overweight, but Cindy says that she had orders from her doctor a while back to trim down.

"I'm only eating 750 calories a day," she moans. "It's so hard! See, I have scoliosis—that's where your spine starts to get kind of S shaped. Well, the scoliosis was putting a lot of pressure on my heart and lungs, just because I was sitting all the time, you know? And that wasn't good for me.

"So the doctors told me to lose weight so it wouldn't be as much pressing on me. I'm pretty short—I'm only five feet, so I shouldn't weigh 136. I'd be taller, but I had a rod put in my back to keep it straighter, and that affects your growth plates or something. So I'm a shrimp. No, the rod doesn't hurt, but I have to sit on something cushy, or my bottom gets really sore!"

She laughs. "And I'm doing pretty good with the diet, except my friends aren't obeying my orders. I told them, 'No matter how much I beg, don't get stuff out of the candy machine for me.' But I lose my willpower and ask them, and they do—they cave right away! They just don't like saying no to me, I guess.

"I've lost enough weight to notice a difference, though. I can tell in my breathing. I used to need about eight breathing treatments a day, and now I only get four—and that's pretty good.

"I really miss some of my favorite foods, though—lasagna, egg rolls, pizza. I have them sometimes, but I have to think of them as treats, only in moderation. I can't pig out like I used to, unfortunately!"

"MY FRIENDS ARE SO IMPORTANT TO ME"

Cindy says that she has many different kinds of friends, both disabled and able-bodied, and they are more important than they may realize.

"I've made lots of friends at school—this is such a great high school," she says. "I mean, there are so many people that are willing to help you, even without me having to ask. All of my classes have been mainstreamed except two, gym and support class.

"But it's so nice to have people around that, I don't know, they'll straighten my foot if it's turned out or adjust something on my chair if it's wrong. Friends will get books out of my bag if I need them. Some of these kids feel more like brothers and sisters than friends. My friends are so important to me."

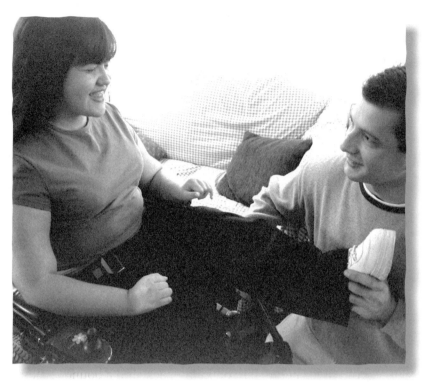

Cindy relies on her family to assist her with her daily routines. Her brother Ian (right) and her other family members help her get dressed, administer her medical treatments, and make sure she receives her medications.

Cindy says that it's nice to be able to confide in her peers, something that's hard to do in her own family, no matter how much she loves them.

"With other disabled kids, you can be more open about stuff you're feeling, I think," she says. "We talk about problems, things we think about. You just get tuned in to what they're thinking."

She frowns. "But sometimes that can be worrisome. I've noticed with this one friend, I think his disability is getting to him. That scares me a little. He's changed, and that worries me. See, he has a type of muscular dystrophy called Duchenne. That's a type where you aren't expected to live much beyond 21.

"Anyway, he just did his eleventh-grade health report—everyone has to do it. You just pick a topic and present it. Well, he did Duchenne, which makes sense, seeing as how he's living with it. But I think it depressed him, reading all about its effects and everything. He doesn't eat much at all; he doesn't seem like the same boy. I worry about him."

"I Have My Down Days"

Cindy admits that while she tries to have a positive outlook most of the time, there are days when she, too, feels discouraged.

"I don't think that's just because of my disability," she shrugs. "I think all kids feel those feelings. But I sometimes feel sorry for myself; I think everyone does. I have my down days.

"I worry about what I'll be doing next year. Will I like college? Will I be able to do the work, to get around? I mean, I think I'll do fine. The community college I'm probably going to attend is really accessible to disabled people, and there's even something called Office for Students with Disabilities to offer support. But it's new and a little scary.

"I'm not sure at all what I want to be. Maybe a secretary or do computer stuff. Steve just got a job doing computer work at a bank, and he's really excited about that. I don't know—maybe every senior thinks about stuff like this without coming up with any answers.

"Other things that get me discouraged is when I think about the stuff I *can't* do, which isn't a good way to think. Like horseback riding—I'd love to do that. In fact, I used to ride at this camp I went to. But that's before the rod in my back, and a bouncing horse wouldn't be the best thing, if you know what I mean.

"Swimming is something else I miss. I used to do that, too. But I can't do it now—my head kind of falls when I get tired. It wears me out too much."

"I've Already Beaten the Odds"

Cindy's voice is much harder to hear now; talking for too long a time is tiring on her lungs. She says that she doesn't like to dwell on the bad parts of her life.

"I've got a lot of good things," she says. "I've got a great family and great friends. My doctors think I'm doing fine. I just take it a year at a time, but I don't think anyone thought I'd do so well. I mean, I've already beaten the odds—I've lived twice as long as they predicted!

"That proves that people shouldn't stereotype, I think. Everyone's different. People have different limits—and they need glasses, or take shots for allergies, or use wheelchairs. To stereotype people by their limits just gets you thinking narrow, you know?

"I wish people would just look at me and see beyond the chair. Kids with disabilities are just normal people. We're normal inside—where it counts, right?"

Epilogue

Since they were first interviewed, a few things have changed in the lives of these four young people whose stories make up *The Other America: Teens with Disabilities*.

Dennis was surprised when his mother called, inviting him to join her and her boyfriend on a trip to Georgia and Florida. He says it was totally unexpected, but he was glad to go. He loved the beaches along the Atlantic Ocean and got very tan. The only thing he felt badly about was missing his dad—although he called home each day. "I worried about him," Dennis says. "We're so close, I knew it would be hard on both of us." Dennis just got a job at a nearby supermarket and is looking forward to earning a little money.

Patrick enjoys summer and wishes it could go on forever. If he has to be at school, he thinks, at least it will be more fun being an eighth grader. He has seen his friend Jerry a few times and enjoyed going to his grandma's cabin and doing a little fishing.

Angie had her surgery, in which doctors broke her legs and reset them. She's spent the summer recuperating, talking with friends, and writing some poetry. She is looking forward to starting school, she says with a sigh, even though it means having to take chemistry.

Cindy has enrolled in college and is looking forward to taking a drawing class. She is still going with her boyfriend Steve; they've been enjoying seeing movies together. Her most memorable experience of the summer was going to camp—a special camping experience for young people with MDA. She says she's really excited about this book coming out. "I've told everyone I know about it," she laughs. "I can hardly wait to show them!"

Ways You Can Get Involved

CONTACT THE FOLLOWING ORGANIZATIONS
FOR MORE INFORMATION ON TEENS WITH
DISABILITIES.

American Disability Association
2201 Sixth Ave. S.
Birmingham, AL 35233
(205) 323-3030
www.adanet.org

The ADA serves as a support group for individuals with disabilities. It provides an exchange of information on disability issues. The ADA makes available children's services, educational and research programs, and charitable services. It publishes *Journal of the American Disability Association* monthly.

Beach Center on Families and Disability
3111 Haworth Hall
University of Kansas
Lawrence, KS 66045
(785) 864-7600
www.lsi.ukans.edu

This organization works to provide families of children with disabilities with the resources and skills to reach full potential. It conducts research on empowering teens and parents of children with disabilities, as well as the efficacy of parent-to-parent support.

ConvoNation
www.convonation.org

This site is an Internet community of sick and disabled teens, a place where they can meet one another, share experiences, and lend support.

Disability Rights Center
4031 University Dr., Suite 301
Fairfax, VA 22030
(703) 934-2020

This is a special-interest group committed to the protection and enforcement of the legal rights of disabled citizens. DRC works to provide information and educational materials to both disabled and able-bodied people concerning the disability rights movement.

Division for Physical and Health Disabilities
c/o The Council for Exceptional Children
1920 Association Drive
Reston, VA 20191-1589
(703) 620-3660 or 1-888-CEC-SPED
www.cec.sped.org

This organization advocates for quality education for all individuals with physical disabilities, multiple disabilities, and special health-care needs who are served in schools, hospitals, or home settings.

For Further Reading

Leo Buscaglia, *The Disabled and Their Parents: A Counseling Challenge*. New York: Holt, Rinehart and Winston, 1987. Excellent bibliography and references.

Al Condeluci, *Interdependence: The Road to Community*. Winter Park, FL: GR Press, 1995. Interesting anecdotes and excellent index.

Helen Hoffa, *Yes You Can: A Helpbook for the Physically Disabled*. New York: Pharos Books, 1990. Although aimed at people with disabilities, this book is a good source for anyone wanting to learn about life with braces and wheelchairs.

PACER Center (eds.), *Living Your Own Life: A Handbook for Teenagers by Young People and Adults with Chronic Illness or Disabilities*. Minneapolis: PACER, 1993. Fascinating anecdotes and exchange of ideas by teens; helpful list of resources.

Milton Seligman, *Ordinary Families, Special Children: A Systems Approach to Childhood Disability*. New York: Guilford Press, 1997. Difficult reading, but fascinating sections on parental roles and differences between cultures in dealing with children with disabilities.

Index

ABOUT THE AUTHOR

Gail B. Stewart is the author of more than eighty books for children and young adults. She lives in Minneapolis, Minnesota, with her husband Carl and their sons Ted, Elliot, and Flynn. When she is not writing, she spends her time reading, walking, and watching her sons play soccer.

Although she has enjoyed working on each of her books, she says that *The Other America* series has been especially gratifying. "So many of my past books have involved extensive research," she says, "but most of it has been library work—journals, magazines, books. But for these books, the main research has been very human. Spending the day with a little girl who has AIDS, or having lunch in a soup kitchen with a homeless man—these kinds of things give you insight that a library alone just can't match."

Stewart hopes that readers of this series will experience some of the same insights—perhaps even being motivated to use some of the suggestions at the end of each book to become involved with someone of the Other America.

ABOUT THE PHOTOGRAPHER

Carl Franzén is a writer/designer who enjoys using the camera to tell a story. He works out of his home in Minneapolis, where he lives with his wife, three boys, two dogs, and one cat. For lots of fun, camaraderie, and meeting interesting people, he coaches youth soccer and edits a neighborhood newsletter.

DATE DUE

362.4
STE

FRANKLIN REGIONAL
SENIOR HIGH
LIBRARY

633053